Getting the most from consultants

A manager's guide to choosing and using consultants

MARTIN WILSON

the Institute
of Management

FOUNDATION

PITMAN
PUBLISHING

London · Hong Kong · Johannesburg · Melbourne
Singapore · Washington DC

PITMAN PUBLISHING
128 Long Acre, London WC2E 9AN

A Division of Pearson Professional Limited

First published in Great Britain 1996

© Pearson Professional Limited 1996

British Library Cataloguing in Publication Data
A CIP catalogue record for this book can be obtained from the British Library.

ISBN 0 273 62048 7

10 9 8 7 6 5 4 3 2 1

Typeset by Northern Phototypesetting Co Ltd, Bolton
Printed and bound in Great Britain by Bell and Bain Ltd, Glasgow

The Publishers' policy is to use paper manufactured from sustainable forests.

Contents

■ ■ ■

v

Preface

■ ■ ■

As a management consultant I am conscious that many clients are unsure how to select consultants and other professional advisers. Those individuals who do appoint consultants adopt a variety of practices in their dealings with them. Some of these practices are helpful, but some are not. Frequently clients do not make the best use of their advisers and, as a result, they do not achieve all the benefits that they could. I hope this book will help managers to realise more of the possible benefits of working with consultants, and thereby help them to achieve greater value for money.

Many managers, especially the owners of small and medium sized businesses, are fearful about using consultants and professional advisers. As a result they struggle with problems that could be easily resolved. I hope this book will help them to overcome their fears and enable them to benefit from the proper use of advisers. There is no need for them to struggle with problems on their own.

Although only the author's name appears on the cover of a book, this masks how much of a team effort a new book is. Without the help and guidance of Richard Stagg, my editor, this book would not have happened. I also have to thank Amelia Lakin, also of Pitman, who kept my nose to the grindstone and ensured that I delivered the typescript on time – it would have been all too easy to submit to other work pressures and delay this book.

When the pressure was on I was especially grateful to my mother, Joyce Wilson, who typed several sections of the book from my rambling dictation. Without that help at a crucial time I would have had to give up this project to concentrate on my day job!

I have to record my particular thanks to my father, Peter Wilson, and a friend and colleague, Tim Stretton, who read the manuscript in a very raw form and made many valuable suggestions. Unfortunately, time and space pressures have prevented me from including them all – so any failings that this book may exhibit are due to me alone.

I also have to thank all those clients, consultants and friends who gave me ideas or case study material. I cannot name you all, but I am grateful for your contributions. I must also include all those other publishers and professional and trade associations who provided me with material for my researches. Again, they are too numerous to list but many are mentioned in the appendices. I hope I have done you justice.

Finally, I must thank Alison, David and Alexandra (my wife and children) for tolerating my absence whilst I was locked away with a computer late into the evening. There were periods when they hardly saw me for several weeks but there were no grumbles. Without such uncomplaining support I could never have completed this book.

Thanks again to everybody who contributed, however small it might have seemed – I appreciate your help and interest.

Martin Wilson

October 1995

1
■ ■ ■

Introduction

The principal purpose of this book is to help you to become an effective buyer of appropriate professional advice. For this to happen, you need to become a good client. By being a well prepared and organised client you will enable consultants to give maximum benefit to your organisation. You will maximise value for money without compromising the quality of the advice that you receive.

This book is a guide to making the most of your relationship with professional advisers and consultants. By making life easier for the consultant and doing much of the straightforward work yourself you will make sure that your consultant can concentrate on using their special skills. No consultant (no good one at least) likes having to undertake basic work that clients could, and should, have been able to undertake themselves. By undertaking such work yourself you will also avoid having to pay a consultant for work that you could do more economically.

Written by a practising management consultant, this book gives an insight into consultants' techniques and motivations. There are things that a client can do to make a consultant more willing, or able, to provide value above that prescribed by the literal statement in the terms of reference.

Finally, this book shares some of the basic techniques used by consultants to analyse clients, their operations and their real needs. Clients can carry out many of these for themselves and thereby give a consultant a more focused brief.

Is this book for you?
■ ■ ■

This book is intended for anyone who has to choose or manage consultants or professional advisers as part of their work. Whilst it will be of particular help to those using consultants for the first time, it will also be valuable for those who have already used consultants. This book will also be of interest to consultants themselves, as by reading it they will discover what their clients are reading.

It is surprising how little most managers know about consultancy and the consultancy process. Most have accepted the stereotypes without challenge. They then wonder why they do not build a viable working relationship or get all the value they might out of their projects. To make a consultancy project work both sides have to approach it with a positive attitude and commitment.

As flatter management structures become more common, more managers and directors have to use consultants to help them with major change and large projects, and to provide them with specialist or technical expertise. The occasional nature of the demand for these resources means that many organisations can no longer justify carrying them in their overheads. Instead they are increasingly turning to external sources – often making use of people who previously provided the expertise in-house but who have now been moved into external consultancies. Many of such organisations' remaining managers are using consultants or other professional advisers for the first time.

Clients and consultants
■ ■ ■

'You can't do good consulting unless you've got a good client.'

These are the words of Michael Younger of the consulting firm A D Little (in *Management Consultancy*, Rassam and Oates). I echo the sentiment. Not only is one able to achieve more in a given time by working with people who are on the ball and know what they (and you) need, but also human nature is such that one tends to work harder and more effectively for clients who are also putting in the necessary effort – you tend to go 'the extra mile' together.

Clients and consultants need each other. Without willing clients there would be no consultancy industry but there would still be all those organisations that currently use consultants. Without consultants the 'client' would have unresolved problems, would continue to make the same mistakes and would let opportunities go unrecognised. On the other hand, without clients consultants would have no role or income and therefore no existence!

3

Who then is the more dependent? I would suggest that it is the consultant; without consultants the 'client' would (and sometimes does) find ways of resolving issues on their own.

Developing successful partnerships

A consultancy project is not a war between client and consultant. Unfortunately some managers, and no doubt some consultants, start the relationship on that basis and then wonder why such expectations are met. A good consultancy project is one where there is a meeting of minds and real collaboration between consultant and client. If the project is working well there will be arguments, often heated and passionate ones, but these will contribute to the project's ultimate success by ensuring that each party has clearly thought through its own point of view.

I have made many long-standing friendships from such projects. Within these friendships we can now bounce around ideas, originated by either party, without there having to be a formal agreement. Out of such debates we originate new thinking that provides new opportunities for the client and, sometimes, new projects for me as a consultant. Such discussions do not have to be forced and they work extremely effectively for both parties.

This relationship is exceptional, but many client–consultant relationships do become close. Much is made of consultants making their clients dependent upon them, but the above example is certainly not a case of client dependency – the client has grown way beyond where we started. Any new project would now be at a much higher level than the original one and both parties would learn from it.

Consultant's Casebook

GROWING TOGETHER

Some years ago I helped a client to plan a management buyout which was abandoned by the main board. We developed a close relationship and five years on I have a very small retainer to provide support on one of their computer systems, a director and I have collaborated on research papers and we both ring each other, from time to time, to try out ideas. I use him as source of specialist information, and he tries out business ideas on me, some of them in relation to his own consultancy work! No money changes hands. I am confident that if there was an appropriate project I would be the first to be called. It is a client–consultant collaboration that has grown into a collaboration of equals. We respect each other's strengths and judgements (and are aware of each other's weaknesses).

Objectives for this book
■ ■ ■

Experienced consultants always seek to make objectives clear before starting any project, seminar or meeting. By doing so they aim to provide a structure and purpose for the exercise. I seek to provide the same clarity of purpose by setting out my objectives for this book. Broadly then, the objectives for this book are to:

- explain the role of consultants and professional advisers;

- show you how to prepare to use consultants;

- guide you through the process of finding the right consultant;

- enable you to undertake some of the work yourself;

- give you the tools to plan and monitor the project;

- help make the relationship as painless and as productive as possible;

- maximise the value for money.

Structure

■　■　■

Objectives

At this point it is useful to set out the structure of each of the chapters in this book. As already described, a key feature of good consultancy, or indeed project management or a procurement exercise, is the existence of clearly stated objectives. So each chapter starts with a statement of what it is intended to provide for you, the reader.

Executive summaries

Similarly, at the end of any piece of work it is good practice to sum up what has been achieved and compare it with the original objectives. Each chapter therefore finishes with an 'Executive summary' of its key points. The summaries have an additional purpose in that they provide quick reference material for times when the pressure is on and you have to achieve results.

Consultant's tips

Throughout the book you will find tips from practising consultants. These can help you, the client, to make the most of the relationship with your consultant by enabling you to understand how they work.

Checklists

Checklists are a key aid to the busy executive. At the end of most chapters there are checklists to assist effective planning.

The Consultant's casebook

Finally, I have included case studies from my 'Consultant's casebook'. These are present for two main reasons: first, the rational, professional reason is to support and illustrate points from the text in real-life situations. Secondly, if we are truly honest, we all like a bit of gossip and to smile at the misfortunes of others! My hope is that the Consultant's casebook extracts will make a useful contribution to understanding by providing a light diversion from the drier procedural sections of the text.

6

Executive summary

This book is to help readers to become more effective purchasers and users of consultancy and other forms of professional advice.

It is aimed at first-time users of consultants, including:

■ owner-managers

■ middle managers

■ newly promoted senior managers

■ directors and others who have never previously used external advisers beyond perhaps their accountant/auditor and solicitor.

It is also aimed as a refresher and a reference for those who have used consultants in the past and wish to:

- avoid previous mistakes in the choice of advisers or the management of consultancy projects;

- update their ideas to reflect current thinking in the way consultants should be chosen or used.

Finally, this book is aimed at a third group of readers: those who are consultants themselves and who wish to know what their clients are reading and thinking.

7

2

■ ■ ■

Why, when and when not to use a consultant

The objectives for this chapter are as follows:

■ to enable you to appreciate what consultancy is all about;

■ to clarify your reasons for needing a consultant or specialist assistance;

■ to explain both clients' and consultants' fears;

■ to enable you to confirm whether or not you need to use consultants;

■ to help you to assess whether you are ready to benefit from the relationship;

■ to ensure that *you* know what problem you are asking the consultant to address.

What is consultancy?

■ ■ ■

Anyone can call themselves a consultant. Consequently the term has been abused by people trying to give themselves spurious authority or credibility. So we get 'communications consultants' (mobile telephone salespeople), 'domestic heating consultants' (plumbers) and, amongst salespeople generally, 'sales consultant' seems to have replaced 'sales executive' as the favoured job title.

I will consider what constitutes a business consultant and the roles they take in more detail in Chapter 3. For now I will use the term 'consultants' to mean any advisers who provide business or technical advice to the management of organisations; this includes accountants, solicitors, management consultants and technical consultants such as engineers, project managers and information technologists.

Consultancy, therefore, is the provision of advice to business by third parties on some form of contractual basis.

Negative stereotypes

> *'They are people who borrow your watch to tell what time it is and then walk off with it.'*
>
> R. Townsend, Up the Organization

Client directors and managers love to parade this type of traditional stereotype of management and other consultants. As with most such generalisations, there is an element of truth in it but it is really a caricature of the truth that may have spawned it. Such stereotypes are rarely based on a single individual or event but are a composite of many. Whilst such negative stereotypes might have been valid at one time, there are few consultants who fit them today. Any that remain are a shrinking minority, because their style of consultancy is no longer acceptable except to the most gullible or inexperienced clients. Hopefully this book will help you to avoid being ensnared by such consultants and will hasten their decline!

Increased acceptance

Despite being the industry that everyone professes to be reluctant to use, consultancy has continued to grow during the 1980s and 90s, even through recession. Consultancy has grown due simply to necessity.

This necessity for consultancy arises from the coupling of two factors: the speed of change in the business environment and globalisation. This combination has created uncertainty amongst business leaders about their ability to adapt to face the future without support. In addition, senior executives are increasingly open to new ideas. The traditional 'not invented here' attitude has become less of a problem as managers have had to accept that becoming 'world class' means learning from their competitors, from other industries and other countries. Consultants are part of the conduit by which that knowledge is shared.

If a client (or would-be client) is prepared to use consultants to learn industry best practice, then they are rather two-faced if they use the criticism that the consultant 'walks off with their watch'. After all, they are using the consultant to tell them the time from (many) other peoples' watches!

Two further factors have encouraged a greater acceptance of the role of consultants:

- Benchmarking, Total Quality Management and other approaches to management *require* managers to accept new ideas and adapt them to their own needs.

- There is a growing number of managers with MBAs in senior positions; many of them will have worked with consultancies at some time in their careers and are therefore willing to accept the role of consultants.

Amongst small- and medium-sized enterprises (SMEs) there

is, perhaps, still some reluctance to use consultants. One reason is that the stereotypical view of consultants is particularly strong there, due to a lack of contact with modern consultancy. However, the reason most often cited is that SMEs cannot afford to use consultants. This may be true, but in the UK (and no doubt elsewhere) there has been some grant assistance for many years to help SMEs to pay for specialist advice. This is in recognition of the need to raise the standard of management and decision making within businesses to enable them to compete in increasingly competitive and global markets.

In part the reluctance to use consultants is a cover for lack of confidence by directors and owners in their ability to select and manage consultants. Hopefully this book will help them to gain the necessary confidence.

12

Nature of consultancy

The increased acceptance of consultancy in recent times is, in part, due to the changing nature of consultancy itself; in turn, the increasing acceptance of consultancy has caused clients to have a greater awareness of what consultants can achieve and so to require consultancy practice to change. There is now much less emphasis on the report-based project, where the consultant comes in, milks the knowledge of client staff, writes a report, sends in the bill and walks away. This is the stuff of the stereotype, but is increasingly rare.

Consultants are having to become much more focused on the achievement of real business benefits. Clients want to see a real return on their investment in consultancy. Lots of jargon is no longer enough; consultants have to be able to demonstrate real understanding of their clients' business, markets and values and to provide solutions that deliver real business or competitive advantage.

Much consultancy is now about enabling clients to find appropriate solutions for themselves. Indeed much of my own work is of this kind. I start by acknowledging that clients should have far more knowledge of their business, their industry and their markets than I can. What I can do is to challenge assumptions and make clients justify their responses and values. I can undertake analysis or research around their knowledge and vision and feed the results into their thinking. I do not let them make glib judgements. I require them to understand their own knowledge and, through analysis, help them to make better, more informed decisions. I often encourage them to implement changes during the process, where these do not cut across the development of the broader strategy.

In the traditional consultancy approach the consultant can be thought of as being like a doctor with the client as a patient. Traditionally the client would be in a dependent position; the new approach requires the client and consultant to collaborate. The consultant listens to the patient's description of the problem (the symptoms) and makes appropriate tests and investigations to diagnose the underlying cause. Having made the diagnosis, a course of treatment is prescribed. If the condition is serious, then the doctor follows up the treatment and monitors its efficacy. Increasingly consultants are following their recommendations through to ensure successful implementation.

13

The important point is that good consultants, like good doctors, do not simply treat the symptoms but seek to identify and treat the real problem. The real cause may be very different from that suggested by the presenting symptoms.

Working as a team with the client

Increasingly clients are demanding that knowledge and understanding of the proposed solution do not walk out of the door when the consultant leaves. They require a transfer of skills and knowledge to their own staff. Involving staff is also key to gaining acceptance of the necessary changes by the client's own people.

The best way of achieving this is for the client and consultant to adopt a partnership approach. The consultant initially works with the client to develop a mutual understanding of the problem. They then work together to find possible solutions and select the most appropriate. How much of the work is undertaken by the consultant and how much by the client will depend on the project. I have undertaken projects where client involvement has been minimal and I have handed over a completely implemented solution. In other cases my time input has been tiny and I have simply provided some direction and challenge of underlying assumptions.

With most projects the consultant should help clients to analyse *their* problem and then work through the process to enable the clients to define the solutions most appropriate to *them*. By working in this way the client's staff are equipped to take the project through to implementation and are able to apply the approach to other similar problems.

14

By involving the client's staff the consultant gives greater ownership of the solution to those who will have to make it work in practice. The skills and knowledge transfer that takes place enhances the individuals' competence and gives them an opportunity to increase their value to their employer (and within the job market).

Fashions

Consultancy is a fashion business or, more accurately, it is a highly fashion-conscious business. The industry is open to accusations of changing its products according to fashion, and there has certainly been a long line of vogue concepts, including:

- business process re-engineering

- total quality management

- the learning organisation.

Whilst these are all valuable tools in the management armoury, they have all been promoted as panaceas by some consultancies. They have then been refined, adulterated and standardised, and turned into general-purpose consultancy products that look remarkably similar to the previous products in new packaging. These management concepts are even more vulnerable to abuse if they can be used to sell computer hardware, as has been the case with business process re-engineering. It would appear that some consultancies are as susceptible to quick and easy solutions as their clients are!

Consultancy products

Many consultancies rely heavily on a product-based approach to selling their services. They develop an approach for solving one client's problem which is successful. They try it on a second client with success – and then they have a product! If they couple the product or methodology-based style with creative thinking and flexibility then there is no problem. Similarly, if they are very selective and only apply it to genuinely similar problems then again it may be a cost-effective approach for the client.

However, you, as a client, should bear in mind the old adage that 'if your only tool is a hammer, everything looks like a nail …'. The consultant with a limited number of products or skills is in exactly that position and will find it difficult to avoid changing a problem to fit their tools. I have seen this happen on more than one occasion at both large and small consultancy practices. If the consultant is sufficiently cynical (or unimaginative, a not uncommon problem even amongst consultants), they use one product on all their projects until they come up with another product or, more probably, re-package their existing product under the guise of the latest management ideas.

Consultant's tip

Beware of consultancies who sell their 'products' too vigorously. Such products are often a mixture of standard methodologies designed to fit a standard solution to your particular business needs. You have to ask whether that is what you want or, indeed, need. Products are easier to sell than is a more specific, considered approach as they are a little more tangible and do not require the consultant to be as creative or closely focused on the client's needs.

Consultant's Casebook

DUPLICATION OF QUALITY MANUALS

Quality systems were a major source of consultancy income for many practices in the late 1980s and beyond. In particular, there was a big rush by many companies, especially manufacturers, to achieve BS5750 (now ISO9000) accreditation – it was seen by many as a way for British industry to achieve Japanese levels of quality. There were also grants of up to two-thirds of the costs of consultancy support to prepare for accreditation.

As a result many consultants jumped onto the band wagon (or was it a gravy train?) and offered support for quality systems development. I came across more than one instance of two clients who had almost identical quality manuals – despite being very different organisations. For example, one company was a sub-contractor manufacturing to their customer's specification; the other was manufacturing their own range of generic products which they sold to wholesalers. Their quality manuals were interchangeable, despite their very different production processes. They had received help from the same consultant to prepare the manual.

Both companies were finding considerable difficulty implementing the systems, and in one case they had taken on an additional person to try to make them work. I involved an associate who specialises in quality systems that are tailored to

16

the specific needs of the client. He managed to reduce the size of the manuals and helped both companies to devise procedures that were no more complex, and that required no more paperwork, than the systems that were in place before the so-called 'quality systems consultant' had become involved. Unfortunately, the clients lost all the savings they had made by using a grant-aided consultant, but they did get workable systems eventually.

A major complaint about ISO9000 has been that it is overly bureaucratic; it is my belief that in many cases this is because 'standard' approaches have been imposed, rather than approaches being designed to meet the individual company's needs. So beware, standard products that have worked elsewhere may not work for you.

17

Why use a consultant?
■　■　■

There are many good reasons for using consultants. Unfortunately there are at least as many bad reasons. If the client's reasons are not good ones then the consultant–client relationship is unlikely to prosper and you will achieve less than you might. Indeed, if the reasons are not valid it is more than likely that the consultancy project will be counter-productive.

Senior management have a responsibility to achieve their business and personal objectives using any of the resources available to them. To do so they use their own staff and other resources (internal and external to the organisation). Consultants are simply part of those resources. If managers have a budget that they can spend on consultants, then they have no excuse for not delivering results that could have been assisted by the use of consultants.

So a key reason for using a consultant is that a manager or management team has recognised that they need help to achieve their business and personal objectives. As with any task they should be seeking to do so:

- on time;

- within budget; and

- with appropriate quality.

Managers therefore need to understand what their objectives are, why they are using consultants, and how they are going to ensure value for money. To do so requires an understanding of their reasons for using consultants rather than doing all the work in-house. Some would say that managers are paid to do what is necessary and that if they cannot then they are not up to the job and should be replaced. However, as we will see, there are many valid reasons for a management team to use consultants rather than trying to do it all themselves.

The wrong reasons for using consultants

18

Let us consider the wrong reasons first so that we can get them out of the way; we can then concentrate on what are important and appropriate reasons for seeking professional advice. Using consultants for inappropriate reasons will be unlikely to achieve positive results and could be positively dangerous to the health of the organisation. If I felt that a would-be client was asking me to take on a project for any of these reasons I would have to turn it down, because I would not have the confidence that I could produce a good result for the client. Apart from the fact that I would not enjoy the work, there is an old saying in consultancy that you are only as good as your last job. It would be foolhardy to take on a project that one knew would not produce a satisfied client. By far the majority of my work comes from referrals by satisfied clients and it has taken me many years to build a reputation that provides that referred work; I am not going to sacrifice it for short-term benefit.

Reasons of ego

Ego is sometimes behind the decision to use consultants, but it does not constitute a good reason for doing so. It usually manifests itself when a senior person wants to tell the world how big he is (it usually is a man): 'I can afford consultants and I use the best' (that is, the most expensive). It is the attitude where image is all. Like flash cars and expensive mistresses, it is more likely to bring the business down than improve its performance. (A partner in a major firm of accountants and insolvency practitioners equates winter tans and Rolex watches with profitable new business – insolvency business!)

To suit internal politics

Unfortunately, external advisers are too often brought in to do work that the client is quite capable of doing, or even has already completed, because of internal political sensitivities. Like many of these wrong reasons, it is an abrogation of responsibility by management. Whatever roles an external consultant should take (a topic to which we will return in Chapter 3), that of scapegoat should not be one. Directors and management have to take responsibility for their own performance and that of their organisation – they are paid to do so and there is a queue of people who would be prepared to take on that responsibility. And the rewards.

19

To force change

Trying to force change is not a reason for using consultants. You might ask, 'Surely much consultancy is about producing change?' It is, but by identifying the changes required and *facilitating* the process. Staff are not stupid; they will recognise when they are being coerced even if management try to shift the responsibility onto a consultant. A consultant has no real authority within an organisation except as an agent of management. Consultancies operate with the support of management and seek to encourage and enthuse staff to achieve results through personality, rather than by direct authority. In the final resort sanctions lie with management, not with the consultant – staff are only too aware of this fact.

To placate staff

Using consultants as a tool to placate unhappy staff is not

only a poor reason, it is also highly dangerous. A good consultant will have their own professional integrity: they will present their findings and recommendations even if they do not meet the client's objective of being a sop to staff (or any predefined result for that matter). The client management is then in a double bind: they have avoided facing the problem themselves and so have given up control; now they either have to act on a consultant's report that contradicts their position or else explain why they are not acting. Staff will draw the correct conclusion – management are seeking a fudge.

Appendix C contains an example of an engagement letter based on work that could easily have been commissioned for such a purpose. It was not, and it was a good job that it was not. The staff, however, expected the result of the review to be all sweetness and light – but life is never that simple. There were many positive findings at an individual level and sensitive recommendations for staff development, but the staff as a group did not like the criticism that was made, as they saw it, of their performance as a team. Even though the consultants explained their findings and stressed the positive, they could not discuss the recommendations with regard to individuals as they could not commit the company to future action. The Finance Director then had the difficult task of selling the proposed course of action to the management team.

To follow fashion

Fashion is not a reason for using consultants. It is the lazy person's approach: it gives an impression of action but it condemns the individual and their organisation to being a follower rather than a leader. If you are not seeking to innovate and lead, then your career is in decline and, if you are allowed to get away with it, so is your business. Remember that the only people who win in the fashion business are those who set the fashion – the fashion leaders – not the fashion victims who are following other people's ideas, too late.

Because you don't know what else to do

I nearly put this amongst the right reasons, but in the end decided it belonged here because if you have no idea of what you want to achieve then you cannot choose the right consultant. As a client, you must have some idea of what you need the adviser to help you to address. It is perfectly acceptable for the problem to be at a high level, provided it is defined: it may be that you need a new strategic direction or vision for the organisation and need an adviser who has the skills and knowledge to facilitate the definition of a new purpose.

Commissioning a consultant without a clear reason can easily become like writing an open cheque. Without clear objectives how will anyone know when the project is complete? In such circumstances it is all too easy to spend a lot of money without any benefit. It is not good for the client, or for consultancy as a whole; but there will always be consultants who are prepared to sacrifice their own reputation and that of their industry for short-term gain. Wise clients do not put themselves in that position.

21

To meet the need for a scapegoat

It is a risky project, so the thinking goes: 'We need to cover our backs, so we'll use a consultant whom we'll blame if things don't work out'. I joke that as a consultant I am a professional scapegoat. I always say that for six months after I leave I will be blamed for anything that goes wrong, even if I had nothing whatsoever to do with it! Whilst I make such jokes I am certain that scapegoating is not a valid reason for using consultants. Furthermore, taking on a consultant on that basis will not create the sort of working relationship that is likely to produce success. By starting with a negative attitude you will almost certainly doom the project to failure. In addition, and this is a crucial point, using a consultant does not, *in any way*, absolve management of their responsibilities. If the project fails, even because of inadequate performance by the consultant, it is still a failure of management. We will look at this more closely in Chapter 6 when we consider the respective roles and responsibilities of clients' managers or directors and the consultant.

With suitable guidance (from this book) you will not start out on a consultancy project for the wrong reasons, and you will manage it effectively and pick up any problems before they lead to failure.

The right reasons for using consultants

A single reason is rarely sufficient cause to use an external consultant, but there are many good reasons that, in combination, justify bringing in professional outside help. These are described below.

Having a clearly stated problem

The key reason, almost a prerequisite, for calling in a consultant is that, as a potential client, you have a clearly stated problem. By 'clearly stated' I do not necessarily mean that you fully understand the problem or can identify its causes or solution. Here are some examples of problems that might be stated by a client:

- We have lost our sense of direction and suspect that our purpose is not understood by directors, managers and staff. We need to re-establish some common vision for the organisation.

- Our business has been built on supplying the armed forces of the UK, but they are shrinking whilst, at the same time, requiring heavy investment in new technology, research and development. We will not be able to compete with the larger suppliers – what do we do?

- We have lost access to our traditional markets because of political changes – we will not have a business in x months.

- We believe that our finance department is comparable to that of other similar companies in terms of the number and quality of its staff, yet they always seem to have their backs to the wall and struggle to meet their reporting and other deadlines.

- Whatever our level of sales we always seem to be short of cash.

- We spend a lot of money on our computer systems, yet they seem unable to deliver the cost and information benefits that were promised.

- Our projects are always late, over-budget and need a lot of post-completion remedial work. We have state-of-the-art project management systems – what is happening?

- We implemented new internal telephone systems, yet customers are still complaining about not being able to get through.

- We have an idea for …

23

At the end of the day, you as the client, have to have some appreciation of the problem you are seeking to address. Your understanding of the problem may not be complete and the possible solutions may be even less clear. However, the consultant will require you to be able to describe the issues and what sort of outcome you need from any advisory or consultancy work.

It is wishful thinking, and dangerous too, to expect your adviser to understand the business and the challenges it faces and then to come up with an instant solution.

Not understanding the causes of the problem

At first glance this reason for needing consultancy almost goes without saying. If you have a clearly stated problem and understand its causes then you are in a position to do something about it. But this is not always true; looking at the problems above, several have clearly defined causes but the client lacks clear strategies of how to respond. Also, you may know what response is required but, for a variety of other reasons, you may not be able to respond without help.

Lacking specialist skills

You may not be able to respond to the cause of a problem because you do not have appropriate skills in one or more specialist areas. This is a common, and very good, reason for using external advice. The advice may be needed at a level much higher than is routinely required by the organisation, and therefore the cost of having it available all the time would be prohibitive.

A common example is in computer systems – an experienced information systems strategist with good business skills may be needed when choosing and implementing new systems. On a day-to-day basis a relatively junior systems supervisor is required to keep the systems running and to undertake modest routine development, perhaps with occasional high-level support from outside. Apart from the cost of having the high-level expertise on the payroll, a suitable person would probably become bored and demotivated, or even worse, disruptive.

This applies to most specialists. It is not simply a question of cost. The potential employer of a full-time specialist has to consider whether there is suitable work to keep those specialist skills up to date. As the case study below shows, it may be valuable to bring outside specialists in from time to time to refresh the expertise of their in-house counterparts.

24

Consultant's Casebook

INVOLVEMENT AND KNOWLEDGE TRANSFER

A chemical processes company had its own team of design engineers with many years' experience of their industry. The chief executive recognised that they were in danger of becoming overstretched by new projects. He decided to call in design consultants to support the work on one of the projects to ease the burden.

Not surprisingly, the reaction from his design team was that they could do the work themselves; they clearly felt threatened by the use of outside help. The chief executive won a measure of acceptance by explaining that the consultants would be there to support them, and by involving the design team in the selection process.

The relationship was a success on several fronts. First, by keeping all projects to their timetables and by managing the designers' workload at a sensible level they were able to maintain quality. There were also several spin-off benefits:

- the design consultants brought in new approaches to the design process itself;

- they also suggested new technological solutions;

- they provided a learning and revitalisation experience for the in-house staff.

As a result the existing staff raised their performance to unforeseen high levels: their expectations of what was possible had been raised.

These windfall benefits turned out to be more valuable, in the long term, than the work done on the original brief, which was well executed by the consultants. The proof of the power of staff involvement and knowledge transfer was that a year or so later the same design team *asked* for design consultants to be brought in, mainly to help the in-house team to develop their skills further and test their own new thinking on independent experts.

A successful relationship for everyone. (And it is not the exception that the stereotypical anecdotes about consultancy would have you believe.)

25

Needing a second opinion or confirmation

Often a management team undertakes an analysis and produces findings that are surprising or challenging. Consequently they are uncomfortable about the validity of their conclusions and wish to have a second opinion before proceeding. If their results were wrong perhaps it could take the company down. In that case it would be foolhardy to proceed without seeking a genuinely objective assessment of the findings. Indeed, that is one of the uses the in-house designers in the above case study had for the outside consultants. They wanted to test their new ideas on an independent expert in the field, someone without any emotional attachment to the developments.

However, be warned: seeking a second opinion *can* be an excuse for management to delay or avoid taking action. It can also be a cover for managers to avoid politically or manageri-ally difficult decisions (see the earlier *Wrong reasons for using consultants* section). If either of these is possible, then the commissioning manager *must* go back and re-examine the justification for bringing in consultants.

Being too close to the problem

As with the designers in the previous case study, all staff, managers included, tend to lose sight of the big picture through day-to-day pressures. Also, as a result of working with the same problems over extended periods, people lose sight of what can be achieved and they accept levels of under-performance as normal. This is not because they are weak or lazy, but because they lose their reference points from other organisations.

26

Consultant's Casebook

EXPECTATIONS

A teacher friend who works with children with learning difficulties finds it necessary to go back occasionally into mainstream schools. He needs to do a spell with children without difficulties every couple of years or so. He does so to remind himself of what 'normal' children can achieve. If he does not do this, he finds that he does not push his 'problem' children hard enough – their under-achievement, relative to most children, becomes his normal level of expectation.

The same is true in any role of life – our achievement is driven by the expectations of ourselves and others. We need to remind

> ourselves what the stars are doing to help us to raise our own expectations. In the current jargon the teacher was seeking a 'benchmark' – often an area where consultants can make a valuable contribution.

Sometimes, then, we need to take a secondment to another organisation to refresh our own perception of what is happening. Often that is not possible, so it may then be appropriate to bring in consultants to help us to see the 'wood for the trees' and to explore the problem. I do a lot of this sort of work, facilitating groups of clients' staff to explore the challenges and opportunities facing their own organisations. As an outsider I can ask the dumb questions that staff would never ask each other – either because they all think that they know the answer or because they are too embarrassed to ask. Often, when required to answer such questions they find that they cannot articulate a response because they do not really understand, for instance, why they do things in a certain way. At that point new insights start to be achieved, from which new solutions can appear.

27

In my experience this is one of the best reasons for using outside help. It keeps the majority of the expertise in-house: the understanding and the solutions are created by the participants. This is an excellent way of producing ownership of the need for change and of the agreed action. It builds on all that expensively-won experience that is already in the organisation. It is also one of the least expensive ways of using consultants. The benefits from one or two days of expert facilitation are enormous – they will provide enough ideas for development and business improvement to keep the management team busy for months!

Not having the resources needed

A common reason, closely related to that of needing additional specialist skills, is that you need extra bodies to undertake a one-off project. However, you must distinguish between contract staff and consultants (a topic we will discuss in Chapter 3). Suffice it to say at this stage that contract staff work under your management and usually to your working hours. Consultants work largely in their own way.

Think about what you are asking the external advisers to do. Are they to take over the project in its entirety and just deliver a fully commissioned solution? If so, is there going to be the opportunity to involve your staff in a meaningful way?

You also have to consider whether your lack of resources is at a management level or with more junior staff. If it is the latter, then it is probably better to use contract staff under your own management. It is usually better to keep the old systems or projects going with contract staff and use permanent staff on the new project. This means that permanent staff feel ownership of the new project and the newly-won experience does not leave as the project winds down.

If your lack of resource is at a management level, then it may be more appropriate to use consultants to support management. However, it is possible to use contract managers who are not consultants and who work on the same basis as permanent staff for the duration of the excessive workload. If there is no advisory aspect, and there are no new skills or expertise required, then I would encourage the use of contract staff or managers – it will be less expensive. If you are venturing into uncharted territory, then an external adviser taking on a combined role of management and specialist adviser is more appropriate.

Lacking information or knowledge

Like a ship's pilot, a consultant can guide a client who is venturing into a new area around the danger points. There are consultants for almost every area of business – cultural, political, management or technical – who can take on this role. It is a very good use of a consultant as it uses their specialist expertise to speed the learning process for the client. By the very nature of this role there has to be knowledge transfer, which I have suggested is the key to the effective use of consultants.

However, beware of charlatans, especially in new technology or areas of thinking that are newly launched. There are consultants offering their services as experts who know little more than you do and who are probably working from the same book. Whilst this can be a problem at any time and in any field, it is particularly prevalent in relation to emerging ideas.

Needing knowledge transfer or insight into current thinking

A key reason for using consultants is to learn from your competitors or to understand more about current developments in an area of knowledge relevant to your organisation. Whilst you will be seeking to keep up to date in all those areas, you may well not have the time to analyse them in any depth. Similarly operational pressures may not allow you time to interpret them in relation to your business needs. You also may simply not have the hard information from your industry or competitors to allow you to benchmark your performance against the best.

Consultants can provide access to such knowledge and experience, without betraying client confidence. They can help you to interpret the difference between your performance and that of your industry in general or in some cases specific competitors. As knowledge transfer is fundamental to this use of consultants it is a sound reason for using consultants.

Needing training and development of staff

The need for knowledge and skills transfer to yourself and your staff is an important part of using consultants and other professional advisers effectively. Whilst it should be an implicit part of any consultancy relationship, there are times when it is the explicit reason for using consultants.

Training and personal development are frequently key objectives in a consultancy project and in Chapter 3 we look at the forms that training and staff development can take. These should be primary skills of any consultant in all but the most technical areas. As with all consultancy, the training should be linked to business objectives and strategy as well as the needs of the individual. It should have clear objectives and, as we will explain later, the results should be tested against those objectives.

Lacking clear goals

It was suggested earlier that you have to be able to state your problem; 'we lack clear goals' is perhaps the minimum acceptable definition of the problem! Such a problem is quite common and most generalist management consultants meet it often. It is not always quite as vague as the heading suggests and it may simply be that you feel that the organisation's purpose is not shared by all staff or understood by your customers or other stakeholders.

A lack of direction often comes about as the result of major change in the industry or its markets, such as privatisation, recession, a new regulatory framework, or major political change (the collapse of the Soviet Union and its impact on the defence industry, for example). The senior management team and staff generally have most of the information and knowledge they need to redefine their goals. What is usually needed is facilitation, and perhaps a bit of help with research into new market opportunities. The client team needs time and space away from the day-to-day pressures to think through the issues; they also need someone to challenge their assumptions and to draw out their existing knowledge so that they can identify the key points. The client may then need help to formulate a plan of action, to take that information away to develop their strategy and then to test the conclusions on an independent person.

Lacking confidence or belief

Very often a problem that is stated as a lack of goals is as much about the client's lack of confidence and belief in their own ideas and abilities. Again the need is for facilitation, possibly coupled with some personal development of key people perhaps by using mentoring techniques and providing them with an external sounding board. At the same time it is usually appropriate to work on team building and the skills needed for the team to provide similar support to each other.

Poor communication or management

Unfortunately this is all too common a reason for using consultants, although that does not invalidate it. The form of the problem and the consultancy approaches that are appropriate would justify a book in their own right. Suffice it to say that this problem requires all forms of external advice and consultancy skills.

Needing a fast or high-quality solution

Sometimes you may want to complete a piece of work more quickly, and possibly to a higher quality, than you can achieve in-house. I am not saying that consultants are always better in these respects than in-house staff – that would be unbearably arrogant. However, a consultant, in their specialist area, will tend to have wider experience, greater knowledge and probably greater access to other sources of expertise, than a typical client's manager. Also, a consultant does not have responsibilities for internal client management and can be expected to have fewer distractions. (The latter may not always be true, but that is what you, as the client, expect to pay for.) As a result a good consultant will often be able to turn a piece of work round more quickly, whilst still maintaining high quality .

Fees, project scope and other issues
■ ■ ■

Within broad terms, any consultant can do what appears to be the same piece of work for a range of fees that may vary in the ratio 10 to 1. Whilst the work might have similar terms of

Consultant's Casebook

NEED OR WANT?

It is very easy for a potential client to confuse what they *want* the consultant to do and what they *need* the consultant to do.

A firm of solicitors had problems with fee-earner productivity and were looking for ways to raise it. They did not have the information they needed to manage how time was spent. I was brought in and asked to buy them a new computer system with a budget of £50,000.

The firm already had a computer system that was fully capable of giving them the information they needed. It had some minor problems that an inexpensive upgrade could resolve. The real problem was that it was not being used properly by the majority of staff.

Furthermore, as I talked to partners about their information needs and working practices it became clear that in many areas fully-qualified solicitors, including partners, were spending a lot of their time on work that was essentially clerical. Work that did not make use of their expensive legal training. To compound the problem the firm were planning to take on another solicitor to do more of this work!

I discussed with the Managing Partner what the firm needed from the consultancy, and we agreed to change the terms of reference to address what was *needed* rather than what they had said they *wanted*. Instead of selecting and implementing a new computer I helped them to make better use of the system they had. More importantly, I helped them to redesign their working practices. As a result the firm spent less than £10,000 on the computer and did not recruit the proposed solicitor. In the first year they saved around £100,000 and freed two partners to take on more high-value work and to spend more time marketing the practice.

The firm carried this approach through to all legal disciplines over the next three years, and produced a substantial increase in business and profitability.

reference it is not the same project in each case. The difference comes from the width and depth of the work. By changing the scope of the work the consultant can often meet a client's fee expectations.

So should you seek the lowest fee from your chosen consultant? No, of course not, but you should be clear about what you get from a wider scope and higher fee. Basically you get more reliable conclusions and more careful recommendations. If the scope is too restricted the consultant will wrap their findings and recommendations in caveats that may well leave you no clearer about the appropriate course of action than you were at the start.

It may be that all you need is a quick review to give you a starting point for your own analysis, in which case a limited scope may be sufficient. However, if you will eventually want the consultant to provide a complete, implemented solution then they will want the analysis stage to be much deeper and wider so that they can be confident that they will be able to deliver the final solution. Both clients and consultants want to find the right scope to optimise the balance between risk and cost. There is no easy way to find the right balance beyond negotiation and discussion.

Fears that cause people *not* to use consultants
■ ■ ■

Clients have a range of fears that prevent them from using consultants. In most cases these fears can be avoided, or at least minimised. They are described below.

Cost

Many clients have heard of the huge day rates that some consultants are paid and know that they could not afford them. Fortunately for the client only a very small proportion of the consultancy profession command such fees. However, good advice is not cheap, so you have to arrange matters to give yourself the most cost-effective solution. This may include: a) not using consultants for work that properly could and should have been done by you, b) using an appropriate basis for the fees and, possibly, c) sharing the consultant's time across a consortium of related but non-competing clients.

Here is an example of the shared consultant approach: the average small shop often cannot justify consultant's fees, but a group of shops on a High Street might be able to use a consultant to address issues common to all of them, such as getting more people into the area and hence into the shops. By working together, not only could they spread the fees, they could also spread the cost of implementation (advertising etc.) and provide a combined front with the local authority and so on.

No guarantee of results

Closely linked to the costs issues is the fear that consultancy gives no guarantee of results. In reality it is often not the cost that is at issue, but whether the results would justify that cost. This can be covered by using results-based fees – these are discussed in Chapter 6.

This book explains that the fear of poor results can be mitigated by a) defining the problem carefully, b) setting clear objectives with measurable results and c) setting these out in sensible terms of reference. By doing this and then following a logical and careful process, you can select the right consultant to work with. All together this should minimise the likelihood of failing to achieve results. Nothing in life is certain except death and taxes; you have to balance the cost of doing nothing against the cost of advice and its implementation.

Also remember that a good result comes from a capable adviser working with a good client. If you as the client are unenthusiastic and leave everything to the consultant, then you deserve what you get. Failure to get results is as much the fault of client management as it is of the adviser, as I hope this book will show. Consultancy has to be a partnership to be successful.

Cultural or political concerns

Many clients worry that the consultant will not be sensitive to the values and culture of the organisation. Choosing a consultant with whom you can work on a personal level and who will respect the organisation's ethos is a key, possibly *the* key, factor in the selection process. An experienced consultant will be able to adapt to most cultures and be appropriately sensitive to your aims and objectives – but bear in mind that sometimes the culture can be the problem and it may be necessary for it to be challenged and justified.

This book stresses the need for mutual respect between client and consultant and encourages you once you have established the technical credibility of your short list of potential advisers to use personal compatibility as a principal determinant for your final choice.

Knowing when to stop

The relationship with a professional adviser should be one of partnership, but within a clear framework provided by well-considered terms of reference. By making mutual responsibilities clear the end of the work should be clearly identified and it should therefore be obvious when the work is complete. A good adviser will be focused on the required results and will not be distracted into addressing or considering peripheral issues.

You also have to manage the relationship and be sufficiently strong-willed to say when you can take over and carry the work forward on your own. Bear in mind the titles – a consultant is an adviser, the client contact is a manager or director. You, as client, are in charge and should be in control throughout the project. You should not in any circumstances delegate responsibility to the consultant.

The terms of reference should identify the end of the project and you should ensure that the scope of the work does not creep. The terms of reference should only be amended (formally in writing) if it is necessary for the work to be broadened or extended. Any consultant who does extra work without such confirmation is undertaking work for which they should not be paid, as it is outside their contract!

Difficulty of identifying a good consultant

Just because a consultant is expensive or sharp or operates from 'swish' premises does not mean that they are good or that they are right for you. The converse does not necessarily hold either – a consultant who is inexpensive, untidy or working from home may still be highly capable. The difficulty of identifying a good consultant worries many clients as they do not know how to decide where they should be looking. This book will help you to find the right consultant for you.

A warning: just because a consultant is cheap does not mean that they will be good value for money. They may simply be inexperienced, perhaps filling in until a job comes along, or even incompetent. Few experienced consultants or advisers need to compete primarily on price. In probably three quarters of my engagements I do not negotiate with the client on fee rates at all and I am certainly nowhere near the cheapest. Do not buy on price or superficial gloss.

> ## *Consultant's tip*
>
> *Buy consultancy, do not be sold it. Buy consultancy when you, the client, have identified the need yourself. Do not be sold it because the consultant sees you as a sales opportunity.*
>
> *If a consultancy firm approaches you suggesting that they can help you and saying things that make sense, then use this as a trigger to analyse your own needs. After you have done this, go out and use the procedures defined in this book to choose the most suitable adviser. As a matter of courtesy you may wish to include the original consultant on the list of those asked to bid for the work – but do not feel beholden to use them. Make the final judgement on what is best for your business.*

Fear of the unknown

37

Many managers and business owners have never used external advisers beyond their accountant and perhaps a solicitor. They have heard all the horror stories about consultants and are fearful about what they might be getting into.

I hope the advice in this book will help you to avoid any difficulties but I can say that most external advisers are straightforward and want to do a good job for their clients. The nature of the work is such that one needs to be highly motivated to succeed as a consultant and such people tend to take pride in their work. There are exceptions, as there are in any field.

Trustworthiness, competence, etc.

The purpose of this book is to help you choose a consultant or external adviser who is competent and trustworthy. It is not as difficult as many make it sound. Most consultants are fiercely proud of their reputation and want to give value for money – I know I get a terrific sense of satisfaction when I produce recommendations that surprise a client but which they accept as giving a real insight into the challenges they face. Seeing the recommendations implemented and achieving real benefits for the client doubles the satisfaction. I am not at all unusual in that.

Failure

If you worry too much about failure then you will achieve little in life. Most success comes from pushing the boundaries just a little further than the competition does. It is the same in sport, business or your personal career: if you do not push at your personal limits you will never be more than mediocre.

Like a rock climber, do what is possible to minimise the effects of failure by using appropriate protection, but do not avoid taking action entirely. By following the processes in this book and adopting a winning attitude of mind you will minimise the chance of failure. After all, management is about managing risk to make the most effective use of resources in pursuit of corporate objectives.

Using external advisers appropriately minimises the risk of failure and may lead to unexpected success. Using consultants increases your own knowledge base; properly used this will allow you to take better and more informed decisions. Whilst success is never guaranteed, failure is more likely to be avoided. If you do nothing when action is needed, failure is guaranteed!

Consultant's Casebook

TAKE DECISIONS

Before my career had started I worked on the shop floor of a small manufacturing company with about 20 people and 3 directors. As I was the only one in the company educated to degree level I tended to be asked to cover for the entrepreneurial managing director in his absence. He always told me to take *any* decisions that *had* to be undertaken to the best of my ability with the best information available. He also said that if it turned out that I'd made the wrong decision he would sort it out when he got back and there would be no comeback on me.

Although I made no *major* mistakes, he was true to his word. It was a very important lesson for me. Now, with more experience, I can see that the risk he was taking was not that large: few decisions are completely irreversible and the benefits of quickly resolved problems are great.

I did not have a name for what this manager was doing until nearly fifteen years later when it started to be termed 'empowerment'!

Change

It is a fact of business life that change is inevitable. Now and in the future the pace of change will quicken, not slow down. Just as with the fear of failure, submitting to a fear of change may also ensure that one fails.

39

The secret is to make changes before your competitors and to make the right changes more often than not. You will not get it right all the time; the key to success is to be right sufficiently often.

Loss of control

This book emphasises that you, as the client, are in control if you choose to be. My argument is that you should take control from the start and maintain it throughout the project. Without clients there are no consultants, but the organisations that would have been clients will exist even without consultants.

You need to take control with a loose rein whilst the work is proceeding as it should. By careful monitoring, not through bureaucracy, you will know when to tighten the rein and take closer control. In the final analysis, control is the client's responsibility; however, most advisers will ensure that a project remains under control in any case.

Runaway costs

All clients worry about the costs of consultancy, but cost is becoming less of a problem. Much project-based advisory work is now undertaken on a fixed-price basis, so the risk of runaway costs lies with the consultant. By adopting appropriate terms of reference and monitoring them properly, the risk of costs running away is minimised. We have all heard the horror stories, but these are usually due to weak management by both consultant and client, and that is avoidable.

Overcoming fears

The fears people have about using consultants are real, but do not let them stop you seeking help if you need it. Failing to address a business problem is likely to be a bigger problem and cause more sleepless nights than the fear of using consultants ever should.

Once you have worked through the selection process and chosen your preferred consultancy firm, discuss your fears with the managing consultant. They will understand them and explore with you ways of avoiding the problem or at least reducing its likelihood. Possible approaches are explored in later chapters; they include taking up references, choosing consultants that you can get on with on a personal basis, using good project management and maintaining communication during the work.

If there is goodwill on both sides then the project will achieve some measure of success. After all, it is in the interest of both the consultant and the client that it should. Remember that without clients there is no consultancy practice – so who is in control?

Consultants' fears

■　■　■

Quite reasonably, clients have fears about using consultants, but the converse is also true. Each time a consultant takes on a new project, especially for a new client, they have their own concerns and fears which the client needs to understand.

Have I been told everything?

Probably the biggest fears that a consultant has to face with every new project are: Have I been told everything? Will what I have promised to do be possible? Are there issues that I have missed or not been told about that will prevent the achievement of the objectives? All these concerns lead to the same question: Have I got the fee right? (Especially if it is a results-based or fixed-price fee.)

It is in the client's interest to be open with the consultant; if the consultant is worthy of the title they will uncover any attempts at deception in any case. If a consultant finds out something significant that they should have been told, then it will immediately create a feeling of mistrust – not a good way to run any project. It is best to be honest.

41

Consultant's Casebook

TELL IT HOW IT IS

A consultant spent two hours with the managing director of a largish financial services company who was seeking help with improving her business strategy. After going through a detailed checklist the consultant had to conclude that the company was doing everything brilliantly. He told the director that he expected them to continue to perform well, to achieve their clear objectives and that he could see no way in which he could help them. The consultant thanked the director and got up to leave ...

The managing director then asked the consultant to sit down with the words 'Well, there are a few things I've not told you ...' Two hours later the consultant left with a contract.

The moral of this tale is not to try to sell yourself to the consultant. Believe a reputable consultant when they say that a

▶

▶

> meeting is strictly confidential. (They do not last long if they are
> indiscreet.) Presumably if you are talking to a consultant you
> have a problem that they might be able to address, so do not try
> to cover it up – it defeats the object of the meeting!

Will I get co-operation?

All experienced consultants have been in the position where
the client's managers and staff have not been co-operative.
Usually they are not deliberately obstructive; rather they are
apathetic or simply go through the motions of working with
the consultant. It is extremely frustrating, as the consultant
simply cannot produce good work. If the lack of commitment
goes all the way to the top, then all the consultant can do is
point out the problem to the client and, if the terms of the contract will allow it, resign from the project. The situation is
entirely avoidable and should be avoided at all costs, as it is
an expensive waste of time for both the client and the consultant.

If there is commitment at the top to make the project work,
then the senior management team and the client have to win
the staff round. Cultural change such as this is difficult and
slow. If it is needed then the original project should be put on
ice until the attitude of staff has (been) changed. Certainly it
is too big a task for most consultancy projects to absorb and
should therefore be treated as a separate, prerequisite project. Most major change programmes require good communication and shared objectives between all staff groups within
the organisation – not at all easy.

Hidden agendas

One of a consultant's biggest areas of concern is the possibility of hidden agendas. All too often the commissioning
managers have issues, as sometimes do staff and other
groups, that they are trying to address, but that they will not

42

disclose to the adviser. Fortunately such issues usually become all too obvious very quickly; however, they leave the consultant with unneeded distractions and often extra work. As before, be honest.

Internal politics

Even if there are no hidden agendas, the internal politics of the organisation can get in the way. Like hidden agendas, the organisation's values and culture are all matters that the consultant has to understand quickly to be effective. The big worry is always that one is missing something important in this area and the whole project could blow up in one's face as a result. Fortunately this does not happen very often, but the apprehension is always there at the start of a project with a new client.

A tendency to believe we know best

There is a tendency for all of us, including a client's staff, to believe that we know best. We often assume that if we did not come up with an idea (with our experience and knowledge of the business and industry) then it is probably not worth considering. Such arrogance is dangerous for the business, especially if one has already identified that there is a problem that could be solved with outside advisers.

You have to make sure that you do not resist the use of consultants for this reason. If I believe a client is taking this view and is reluctant to use consultants I will probably decline the work: the client will be almost impossible to satisfy and they will denigrate any recommendations that are made as 'obvious' or 'impractical'. The fact that they have not come up with the suggestions and, even worse, have failed to act on any ideas, will usually escape them.

Consultant's tip

There is still a considerable tendency for management to be problem-solving rather than opportunity-seeking. This seems to be particularly true of owner-managers and middle management in large organisations – they tend to be conservative and do not like change. Competitive advantage comes from seeking and taking advantage of new opportunities and usually requires change.

Unfortunately there are still many consultants who prey on this and provide simplistic small improvements that give everybody the satisfaction of spurious achievement. Such consultants are part of the problem. Addressing the symptoms rather than innovating to take advantage of a bigger opportunity is all too common. It is easier than being creative.

Do not be satisfied with modest or short-term 'solutions'; look for significant benefits.

44

Ownership of the project
■ ■ ■

For any project to be really successful there are a couple of ingredients that are essential. The first is high-level commitment. The board really has to believe in the work so that they will support it wholeheartedly. They should offer active support that is visible to everyone concerned or affected by the work. If such support is not there the commissioning managers should question very carefully their motives and the possibilities of success without that backing. Can they really take the project through to fruition, or is it just going to be yet another failed initiative?

Such genuine high-level support will encourage support by all staff. However, the staff will need to believe in the project for themselves. The second ingredient, therefore, is involvement. Staff cannot be led like sheep, but have to be involved in the process, without the management team giving the impression that they are seeking to make decisions by consensus (simply not possible where there are more than two people). Involvement can take many forms but should seek to use the knowledge and experience of all staff.

When I run business planning workshops or brainstorming sessions with staff groups I tell them that I want to know the problems, ideas and solutions they discuss amongst themselves over coffee or in the pub at lunchtime. Such ideas are valuable in themselves, but they also provide an insight into the real issues. They come from people who have to make the systems work that others, perhaps without real understanding, have imposed. If that advice is sought and seen to be used then it will provide real encouragement to make the project work.

Such advice-seeking sessions should not be one-off, but should be part of a programme that incorporates feedback on what happens to the ideas generated. With business planning work we usually collate everybody's thoughts and share them amongst all groups without identifying any individual's comments. In large hospitals doctors have been surprised to see that they are not the only ones worried about patient care and that it is also high on the list of concerns of domestic staff and porters. (Actually they often place it higher than doctors do.)

It is beyond the scope of this book to cover creating 'ownership', as there have been many books on that topic alone. Managers and consultants should be aware of the need to do so and should find means appropriate to their own organisation. The drivers of ownership will be different for different groups and cultures.

When not to use consultants

■ ■ ■

There are times when influences, often external ones, make it inappropriate to use consultants. These situations are described below.

45

Initiative overload

There are occasions when an organisation finally decides to take action and asks its managers to act. Unfortunately, if the work is not co-ordinated with other projects it can lead to initiative overload and lose the support of staff. Even worse, the many different initiatives may pull against each other, causing staff to become frustrated as their priorities keep changing and they are confused as to what is expected of them. At this stage it is only appropriate to involve consultants in one role – to pull everything together and to reconcile conflicts in the existing projects. It is the only role I would take; I would walk away from anything else.

The case study below highlights the need to get the *real* problem clear at the earliest possible stage. Initiative overload can only come about if there is inadequate communication coupled with inappropriate decision-making processes. It is best to address those issues first so that everyone can see their role in the other changes that will follow.

46

Consultant's Casebook

34 PROJECTS, 3 CONSULTANCY FIRMS AND ZERO DIRECTION

I met an organisation with a new chief executive who had, quite rightly, decided that major changes were needed. She had organised an intensive two-day workshop for her senior managment team to brainstorm a new direction and to identify the key changes that were required. As a result she encouraged her functional heads to plan projects to address the key issues they had identified. This they did, and by the time I was invited to bid for some work, they already had three other consultancy firms involved.

Staff were shell shocked. They were being pulled in all directions, priorities changed by the hour and the situation was having a serious impact on the work of the organisation. To all intents and purposes staff had given up on the change programmes – they were not even making a token effort. They knew it was futile. Initially they had been keen, as they knew change was necessary, but they were soon overwhelmed. Sickness rates were up, staff turnover was increasing and customers were complaining.

It was a case of initiative overload – there was too much happening for anyone to understand how it all related. There were projects to address problems caused by other projects. In total there were 34 projects going nowhere. There was no co-ordination, no project management and the consultants had free rein. They were taking fees for work that was never going to give benefits.

After discussions I told the chief executive, who was showing serious signs of stress, that there was only one project I was prepared to take. I would only work for her if I was given the task of co-ordinating all the work that was going on. I would also require the authority to kill any project and remove any consultants who were not delivering. I was not surprised the chief executive did not feel able to give me such a brief – she still hoped that the huge expenditure could be justified by achieving some success, somewhere. She knew her job was on the line if she did not pull something out of the hat but it was far too late.

Less than a month later she had been replaced by a more experienced chief executive who had been seconded from elsewhere. He killed all the projects and sacked the consultants, claiming damages for non-performance from them. But the damage had been done to staff morale, performance and budgets. Within six months the organisation disappeared as it was merged into a similar organisation nearby.

External and environmental pressures

One has to be very careful when an organisation is facing major change or external influences. These include merger, demerger, privatisation and changes to industry regulations. Keeping staff focused on the project in these circumstances is difficult unless it is clearly related to the big challenge. Similarly, effort could easily be wasted if a new structure or regulatory framework has different requirements. Do not start making changes that might be overridden by other, bigger, wider-ranging changes.

Different departments or managers pursuing own agendas

There may be times when the tensions within the organisation are such that each department is trying to use any consultancy project for its own ends, or even commissioning different consultancy firms with conflicting terms of reference to achieve their particular aims. This is expensive and clearly a sign of an overriding issue that needs to be resolved before the organisation can hope to move forward in any co-ordinated way.

Such a problem is one that management itself has to address; consultants cannot do it as they do not and should not have the authority to take the necessary action. Advisers can assist by acting as honest brokers or go-betweens. Consultants can also act as facilitators for discussions to get to the bottom of the issues causing the tensions.

Similarly, if the culture of an organisation is in a state of turmoil and people do not believe that there is a clear direction, that is also a problem that should be addressed first. Will staff be largely supportive of the proposed work? If they are not, for whatever reason, then this needs to be resolved before spending money on consultants. Communication problems within an organisation can cause problems for major consultancy work as they can lead to mistrust and false rumours. To be fully effective, all consultancy requires the support of staff at all levels. Make sure that support is there before recruiting consultants.

Such problems, if they exist, need to be resolved before any other project is started.

Preparing to use consultants
■   ■   ■

Once you have established your need to use consultants, you should prepare carefully. This section suggests how to do this.

Think of the future

Use consultants to take you into the future; do not simply focus on the immediate problems of today. Be creative – do not accept simply tweaking the status quo. Customer expectations and competitive pressures are changing rapidly and if you do not move forward quickly then you will lose ground to your competitors. Incremental change that was acceptable a decade or so ago is no longer fast enough. All organisations need to make large changes to respond effectively, and need to make them frequently. By using consultants in this way you should get a better return on your investment in time and money.

Formulate a business plan

Any organisation, whatever its objectives, should have a formal written business plan. It need not be a long document but it should contain the following: a statement of the organisation's purpose, 'vision' or 'mission', the associated objectives and how achievement of those objectives will be measured. It should be used as a working document by all managers and the board, at least.

49

Normally the business plan will look forward in detail for the next year and in summary for the following two to four. It should be updated each year and its contents should be widely shared throughout the organisation. Its preparation should be based upon the ideas and recommendations of as wide a group as possible.

Prepare the ground internally

It will be necessary to prepare the ground with other managers and staff. They will need to understand what the consultants are being brought in to do, what the expectations are for the project and the impact that it might have on the people concerned.

Everyone needs to be encouraged to express their concerns and to contribute, as far as possible, to the work. It should be stressed that the consultants are there to advise and that management will have to decide if and how they will implement any recommendations.

Do not lose sight of the big picture

Finally, although a problem may be large, try to avoid breaking it up into small pieces. Large problems tend to have wide-ranging implications and a fragmented approach will miss many of the connections. The result is likely to be a set of solutions that is less effective than one cross-disciplinary solution produced by a single project.

Instead of breaking the problem into a series of separate, perhaps departmental or functional projects, treat the whole like an onion. Peel away a layer at a time, working across all disciplines and gradually getting deeper and deeper into an understanding of the whole. Solutions will develop at each level and it will be much more manageable than many separate pieces of work.

Executive summary

Although there are many consultancy stereotypes, there is growing acceptance and use of external advisers. This appears to be because the old certainties in business have disappeared whilst the pace of change continues to accelerate. Organisations need advisers to share best practice and to help them learn from their competitors.

Consultancy is changing from a prescriptive role to one that is facilitative and that helps clients to find their own solutions. This provides the necessary skills and knowledge transfer to allow the client to carry the work forward.

However, consultancy has been increasingly fashion conscious and you, as a client, have to see past the superficial gloss of many consultancy 'products'. You need to look to the benefits that will be achieved, rather than to the consultancy process itself.

There are many good reasons for using consultants but you have also to be careful that you do not use external advisers for inappropriate reasons. Using consultants inappropriately is likely to be counter-productive. The fears of both clients and consultants can also get in the way of successful consultancy. We need to understand these fears and address them in the new partnership approach to consultancy – with goodwill and proper selection they can be all but eliminated.

If you are to use consultants there is work that needs to be done to prepare for doing so. Before you engage an adviser you have to be clear about what you need and have the information available that the consultant requires to understand you and your problem.

Checklist

1 Do you understand why you need consultants? Is it appropriate to use consultants?

2 Are the reasons valid? Honestly?

3 Do you have commitment from the highest level in the organisation?

4 Can you take staff and other managers with you? Will they 'own' the results?

5 Is the timing right? Are the senior management, staff and the organisational structures prepared?

6 Is the external environment right? Are there no major external factors, such as merger or regulatory changes, that will overwhelm the proposed project or potentially render it invalid?

7 Do you have the key documents available? (Corporate strategy, business plan, existing marketing plan, for example.)

8 Have you defined the problem, at least in broad terms?

3
■ ■ ■

Meet the consultant

The objectives for this chapter are as follows:

- to explain what a consultant is;
- to enable you to recognise what a consultant is not;
- to describe the many roles a consultant can take;
- to explain what makes a consultant tick;
- to give you some information about consultancy regulation.

What is a consultant?
■ ■ ■

Consultants are different things to each client and will change their role to match the needs of each project. A good professional adviser will have a wide, cross-disciplinary view over many functional areas so that they are able to recognise connections with other specialisms. At various times most consultants take on many of the roles described below and others as well.

Adviser

First and foremost a consultant is an adviser, usually in one or two specialist areas. They may specialise in functional areas, such as information technology, finance or design, or they may specialise in an industry or sector, say, health care, engineering or Asia. The consultant will share their expertise with the client and help the client to apply it to their specific needs.

This advisory role is often preceded by the consultant taking on a diagnostic or analytical function to determine what advice is needed.

Diagnostician

Often the first role a consultant takes with a client is to discuss the symptoms and the client's perception of the problem. The consultant then seeks to diagnose the real cause and nature of the problem. This is done by examining the available facts and then conducting tests to rule out or confirm possible causes. The procedure is much the same as that followed by a doctor, although the details are rather different. As with a doctor, some business advisers are 'general practitioners' who diagnose and 'treat' the more common business problems and who call in specialists when the problem is outside their competence.

Both doctors and business consultants recognise that the presenting symptoms may not be the problem itself, but merely an indication of something wrong elsewhere. Accurate diagnosis is therefore important; a good consultant will not jump to conclusions but will make careful investigations before deciding on a course of action.

Consultant's tip

Avoid consultants who tell you that your problem is 'the same as a problem we had at ...' especially if they do so at an early meeting. They are missing the all important diagnostic step and are likely to force their standard solution onto your particular problem, whether it fits or not!

55

Analyst

Diagnosis is included within analysis, but the role of analyst goes much further. Analysis involves understanding a wide range of relevant information. Much of this information is relevant to the problem but is not part of the diagnosis; it is information that needs to be understood to formulate a course of action in response to the diagnosis.

Many advisers undertake ongoing analysis (both formal and informal) that is not related to specific projects; they do this as a means of maintaining and enhancing their knowledge. All good consultants take their own personal development very seriously and spend a considerable amount of time and money on it. They will read widely within and around their specialist area and may undertake formal research or training and education. Many professional institutes (including those of solicitors, accountants and doctors) require their members to undergo a minimum amount of continuous professional development (CPD) or training to maintain their qualification. Many other professional bodies encourage CPD and may well make it compulsory as their scheme becomes more developed; amongst this latter group are the Institute of Management and the Institute of Management Consultants.

Researcher

Closely allied to the role of analyst is the business adviser's function as a researcher. Even the best consultants do not know all that there is to know about their field or the industries in which they work. That would be impossible. However, a good consultant will be an effective researcher and will know where and how to find any required information.

Most of the effective consultants I know are particularly strong in this area. They build and maintain a strong network of experts whom they can call upon for advice when necessary. Some of these experts may be inside their own organisation – the very large consultancies encourage this networking on a global basis – but many will be external. For instance, I have taken the positive decision in my own fairly small consultancy practice not to build a large, permanent organisation with many in-house specialists, but to form a more dynamic organisation that uses a large network of third-party experts, coupled with modern technology, to achieve the same sort of result.

An effective consultant will know where to find, quickly and reliably, almost any sort of information relevant to their field. As with many things, trust the adviser who says, 'I don't know the answer but I can find out,' rather more than the person who claims to know it all.

Teacher

An increasingly important role for professional advisers is that of teacher. As consultancy professionals move from a prescriptive style of consulting to a more facilitative approach, then their skills as a teacher grow in importance. Clients are increasingly seeking skills and knowledge transfer; they want to be able to do similar work in the future with much less outside support. Many business advisers will, on occasions, become teachers or trainers and run formal classes or seminars to pass on skills or knowledge in their particular field.

The consultant's teaching function often starts at a very early stage of the relationship with a prospective client. Frequently the adviser has to provide guidance on how to use consultants. Indeed, this book is part of such a teaching process.

Consultant's Casebook

CONSULTANT AS TEACHER AND RESEARCHER

One should be able to take a consultant's competence for granted, but this is not always the case. The following is a true story (I was not the consultant!):

A client was becoming increasingly uncomfortable with a consultant they were using – he did not seem to be on top of his subject. One Friday evening they reached the decision to confront him the next week, and probably to terminate the contract.

On Monday the consultant came in and, with a completely straight face, told the client manager that progress on the project might get a little rocky as a problem had arisen: the library had recalled the book he was using! The project was terminated there and then with no redress.

A consultant often has to be a teacher, and it is often said that a teacher should be 'a chapter ahead of the pupil' (so they do not make assumptions about the pupil's knowledge). In this case the consultant had taken this idea too literally and was being very unprofessional. By not doing his research and understanding it fully before starting the work, he had failed on the first of the key judgements any consultant needs to make. 'Am I competent to take on this work?'

This consultant had not made that decision correctly on several counts. He was not competent in the field, his research was not

> competent, and consequently his teaching, diagnostic and
> advisory abilities were flawed.

Mentor

Mentoring is not the same as teaching, although it requires
many of the same skills. The relationship is not one of
teacher–pupil, nor is it supervisory; it is more of a peer relationship. When mentoring is working well the mentor gains
as much as the person mentored.

The role of mentor is complex and highly individual – each
person will handle it in their own way. A mentor provides
encouragement and motivation through guidance, advice and
support, as someone outside the organisation. It is essentially
a service provided on a one-to-one basis, usually over an
extended period, with contact being occasional and often at
the request of the person being mentored. The mentor acts as
a sounding board and tries to help the client find their own
solution by challenging their thinking and assumptions. The
mentor asks questions to lead the client to their own conclusions, not those of the mentor. As the mentor often has wider
experience than the client, they will also share that
experience and use it in support of the client's decision
making. In any case, both mentor and mentored will pool
their knowledge, expertise and thinking, so that the person
being mentored can make a better informed decision *of his or
her own.*

Facilitator

Closely allied to the role of mentor is that of facilitator; it is a
role that consultants are required to take on with increasing
frequency. Both clients and consultants recognise that there
is considerable expertise within organisations. Unfortunately, traditional organisational structures are not capable
of extracting and using that knowledge. Facilitation is one

means of liberating this expertise. Its goal is to make groups within the organisation aware of what they know and to help them to convert it into effective action in support of business objectives.

Whilst a mentor works with one individual at a time, a facilitator works with groups. This is usually done by holding meetings of the whole group, but it can be spread over time with individuals or small sub-groups, often supported by meetings of the whole group. As with most aspects of consultancy, there are few hard and fast rules; flexibility is essential in meeting the needs of the client.

The best facilitation recognises that senior members of any group do not have a monopoly on wisdom. Facilitation aims to draw on the group's knowledge and imagination and to build towards a shared vision and common goals. Good facilitation is perhaps the most effective means of achieving knowledge transfer and of giving ownership of the proposed solutions to the participants. After all, the solutions are indeed their own; all the consultant does is to ask the dumb questions to which everyone wants answers but which they are too embarrassed to ask!

Apart from gently steering the group on a course that addresses the priorities, facilitation is also about one of the most important parts of any adviser's job: the challenging of assumptions behind current or proposed action. Often those assumptions are the received wisdom ('we've always done it that way' or 'because it is') and nobody has revised them in the light of modern conditions. The consultant uses facilitation to unblock the client group's thinking, to keep the discussion focused on the issues in hand and to handle some of the people issues.

Interpreter

I have often said that one part of my work is to act as an interpreter. The languages involved are, respectively, that of the technical specialist and that of the generalist business man-

59

ager. In my case, I usually interpret between information and other new technologists and business managers. I can interpret both ways: put the technical issues in a business context and explain the business objectives in a way that is relevant to the technologists. The specialisms are not important; interpreting can take place just as well between finance specialists and clinicians in a hospital.

All but the most technical consultancy work requires multi-disciplinary skills to build bridges between functions. Increasingly, businesses are recognising that the traditional functional structures are no longer appropriate if they are to meet customers' expectations. Even the technical consultant has to be able to talk, without jargon, to finance, marketing, production and other staff, to explain the issues, challenges and the reasoning behind proposed technical solutions. Acting as an interpreter will be an important function of professional advisers for the foreseeable future.

Source of specialist expertise

If you ask most people what makes a consultant, they will usually, after they have exhausted the stereotypes, describe some form of expert. They will often cite technical specialists, such as computer consultants or engineers. Of course expertise goes much wider; there are business advisers and consultants with specialist expertise in almost every area of business and related fields. So there are economists, accountants, marketing people, advertising agents, designers, ergonomists, psychologists ... an endless list. The skills do not have to be functional or technical; there are consultants who provide knowledge and expertise in particular industries, such as the automotive or electricity industries, or in geographical areas, such as Scotland, Africa or Eastern Europe.

There are successful consultants providing specialist advice and insights into almost any field that one can imagine. If it is an area of knowledge that people need, however occasionally, there will be someone who has both the knowledge and willingness to act as a consultant. However, technical or specialist expertise is not enough on its own as we will explore later.

Project manager

Consultants routinely operate as project managers to deliver results for both their own firm and for the clients. Consultants are project managers for most of their work.

To succeed as consultant one has to be a reasonably effective project manager; so by the time a consultant has become a Managing Consultant and is running consultancy projects they should have well developed project management skills. A Managing Consultant not only has to manage their own firm's resources to ensure profitability, they sometimes have to manage resources on behalf of the client. In such cases the resources will include staff over whom the adviser has no formal authority; they therefore have to achieve results by encouragement and through their own enthusiasm, commitment and personality.

Innovator

> *'But every organization – not just businesses – needs one core competence: innovation'*

These are the words of Peter Drucker, perhaps the century's leading thinker on management issues, writing in the January–February 1995 issue of the *Harvard Business Review*. As external advisers are frequently brought in to assist organisations to respond to a rapidly changing world, then it follows that a key skill of a consultant is the ability to innovate. That innovation can be in technology, in the organisation of the business, its staff and its processes, in markets, or in other aspects of the organisation.

Innovation has to be directed towards redefining and/or supporting corporate objectives, so frequently the consultant has to act as a bridge between functional areas or to relate technology, the business needs and the people issues. Hence, apart from creative skills, a consultant also needs a breadth of vision so that they can see opportunities and the issues beyond their own specialism.

Prophet

Vision is a precursor to innovation and forms the role of the prophet. Innovation requires an idea for a new way of doing things and a belief that there is a solution. The external advisers who stay ahead of current thinking in their field can provide that vision for their clients. By knowing about ideas that are in an early stage of development, consultants can help clients leap generations in management thinking or technology and thereby gain competitive advantage.

62

Counsellor

The consultant also has to curb wild ideas and bring reality to bear. They have to help the client to cut through the hype associated with many new ideas or products. (In fact, if the ideas are at the hype stage then they are hardly visionary as they are very much in the public domain.) The consultant has to couple vision with pragmatism and to recognise what is achievable *for this client*. Different clients will be at different stages of development, and their capabilities will be different: one client's generational leap will be another's incremental improvement. The consultant has to help the client to dream the *possible* dream.

There is another aspect of counselling that can be very difficult: very occasionally a consultant will come to the conclusion that the commissioning manager (or another very senior person) is the problem, or is at least part of it. If that person is one of the senior management team, then the consultant may have to take them on one side and, very sensitively, explain the problem, the individual's role in it and how they might address it. If the person is junior to the commissioning manager then it is that manager who has to take the appropriate action, perhaps with the advice and support of the consultant.

This situation is not common, but when it happens it can really test a consultant's integrity. I have had it happen to me and, in one case, the person concerned had commissioned me and was responsible for authorising my invoice! I had to tell him the truth, talk it through over several discreet, off-site meetings and guide him into a course of action to address the difficulties. I did get paid and he retained me for nearly two years to act as his mentor – he developed considerably, addressed the problems and was consequently promoted.

Sometimes it is not possible for the person concerned to make the necessary changes. Then all the adviser can do is to make suggestions for mitigating the problem by changing responsibilities, and leave it to the senior management team to sort it out.

63

Diplomat

As some of the previous roles have indicated, an ability to be tactful and sensitive is amongst the most important assets for a consultant. It is not uncommon for an adviser to have to tell a client something that they will not like. Depending on the relationship and the effect desired on the client, the consultant may be blunt and provocative, or diplomatic.

For example, telling a client that they have just spent a year's profits on equipment that is unsuitable or explaining that their values are not compatible with the market are both situations that require sensitive handling.

If your adviser tells you things you do not like, remember that you asked them to do so. Do not shoot the messenger – address the problem.

Conscience

Finally, a key role for an external adviser is to act as a conscience. You should expect a consultant to be blunt at times and sometimes provocative. Remember George Bernard Shaw's words (in *Maxims for Revolutionists*):

> *'The reasonable man adapts himself to the world: the unreasonable one persists in trying to adapt the world to himself. Therefore all progress depends on the unreasonable man'*

External advisers are asked to be an unreasonable person on their client's behalf, so do not blame them when they tell you things you do not like about yourself, your staff and your organisation. You asked them to take on that job. Use the provocation as a spur to make progress.

What a consultant is *not*

■ ■ ■

In this section we consider two roles that are inappropriate for consultants.

Member of staff

A consultant is *not* a member of staff, at any level. If the person works as a member of staff then they are not working as a consultant, but as temporary, freelance or contract staff.

What separates a contractor from a consultant? There are many suggestions; one is that a consultant is anyone who travels more than fifty miles to work and who carries a briefcase! However, realistically, a better measure is who determines when and how the work is performed. A consultant is essentially self-managing, and will determine when they work, where the work is performed and the approach they take to the work. The terms of reference for the project will provide a framework in which those decisions will have to be taken, but the negotiation is the client's only real input to the management of the selected consultants. A contractor, on the other hand, will work hours specified by the client and will, generally, be managed by a manager on the client's staff.

Sometimes a senior manager or even a director will be required by a client to cover illness or whilst a vacancy is filled. Such interim managers may often come from consultancy firms and may use many of their consultancy skills. However, in such circumstances they are not working as a consultant but as a manager or director. Although they may be consultants by profession, they are managers because they are taking decisions on behalf of the client. Generally a consultant will advise, and may make some decisions along the way, but the key decisions *must* be taken by the client. The client's management team will be around long after the consultant has left. They will therefore have to bear the consequences of their decisions and have the responsibility of ensuring that they maximise performance, however measured. A consultant should not take key decisions on behalf of a client. It is not part of their role and can lead to other problems.

65

Shadow director

Many professional advisers should be very careful about being considered shadow directors. Shadow directors are people who are not registered as directors but who effectively act as directors, to all intents and purposes taking on the responsibility of directors. The law relating to shadow directors is intended, in part, to prevent people disqualified from running a business from doing so by proxy.

In normal circumstances, being judged to be a shadow director is not a problem, but in the event of any difficulties the individuals can be held to be responsible in the same way as formally appointed directors. There can also be conflicts of interest as a director (shadow or otherwise) should not act in certain roles, for instance as an auditor.

Key skills of a consultant
■ ■ ■

Consultants need special skills. These are described below.

The ability to be candid

Consultants are recruited, in part, for their judgement; the key judgement they can make is whether they are competent to undertake the work on offer. This facility to be candid with themselves must be a key ability of any professional, but it is especially important for those acting as business advisers.

Inter-personal skills

Surprisingly, the next most important skills of a consultant, technical or otherwise, are not their specialist skills but their inter-personal abilities. The technical skills need to be sound, of course, but they are not the most important. It is the inter-personal abilities that sway the client. Surveys of the important factors for customers of professional service companies list 'affability', 'availability' and 'affordability' way above 'ability'. The reason is quite simple: the average client does not have the specialist knowledge and experience to judge the technical quality of the work. So by choosing a firm with an established reputation, good references or on some other basis the client takes the technical quality as a given. For example, how many people can judge the quality of treatment provided by their family doctor or a hospital consultant? Most people assess their doctors by other, arguably peripheral, measures. These might include the ease of getting an appointment, their 'bedside manner' or whether they are members of the same golf club!

The most important skills, then, are the inter-personal ones. If one considers the roles asked of consultants it can be seen that these are essential. Most of the roles require effective consultants to be people-oriented with listening, communication and teaching skills. They need to be able to empathise with their clients, client staff and managers, and to be able to give them difficult news sensitively.

When change projects (such as re-engineering) fail, whether consultancy supported or not, it is often because effort only goes into the technical aspects. The processes and the technology are understood, but surprisingly little is known about the people issues. The 'hard' issues are fully addressed; the 'soft' people issues are glossed over because the people leading the project are technicians (finance, marketing, information technologists etc.) rather than people-oriented. These 'soft' issues determine the success or failure of most projects however technically competently they are implemented.

More consultants with a leaning towards psychology as well as their other specialist skills are needed to address this problem. Without them client managers and staff will always have some distrust of consultants. Unfortunately, this is unlikely to happen quickly because commissioning managers tend to be technicians themselves and will tend to recruit consultants in their own image.

Even when dealing with technical aspects, consultants need more than simply to understand them, apply them or even explain them to clients. They need to be able to analyse a problem and apply the relevant parts of their technical expertise, as well as to identify what other technical knowledge they require.

The ability to innovate

Finally, in my view one of the most important abilities of any consultant, there is the ability to produce innovative but practical solutions. The accelerating pace of change in all business environments means that minor improvements are no longer sufficient. Consultants, and clients, need to find major performance gains to stay with the pace. These will not come from working to strict methodologies; they will only come from innovation. Consultants must be more than journeymen; they must posses the capacity for creative thinking, coupled with all the other consultancy skills.

Consultancy organisation and practice
■ ■ ■

The consultancy industry

Consultancy, in all its forms, is a knowledge-based service

business. It has low start-up costs and, initially at least, low overheads. Although many assume that a home-based business is cheaper than an office-based one, this is not necessarily the case. For a professional operation the differences are not as great as one might imagine, because consultancy is labour-intensive and therefore salaries are the major part of the costs. If a consultant works from home, do not automatically expect lower fees.

Consultancy differs from many businesses in that its products are intangible and, to a large extent, have to be taken on trust – although, as I show in this book, there are ways of minimising the risk.

The professional advice industry changes rapidly, so consultants have to spend a considerable amount of their time keeping their knowledge and skills up to date. This also means that consultancy firms change rapidly: products have to change with new thinking, and the standing of an individual firm can change quickly if key staff leave. Many new firms are formed by groups leaving a larger firm to create new, usually specialist, consultancy practices. If a key team leaves a firm with a high standing in a particular field, that firm can lose a hard-won reputation overnight to the new start-up.

Why do people become consultants?

My first reaction is, 'Heaven knows'! Being a consultant is difficult, demanding and plays havoc with one's social life, but it has its compensations for a certain type of personality.

Having to face new challenges is a way of life for consultants, so to be successful they have to be self-starters. Consultants need to be able to tolerate loneliness and long hours that put pressure on their social lives. They also tend to have a personal attitude that commits them to achieving a result whatever it takes.

Consultants must also have other attributes: they have to be independent without being a maverick (well, not too much of a maverick!); they have to have the intellectual capability to be able to cope with both micro and macro issues. Like all creative people, they have to be able to see the obvious before anyone else can and then make connections that are less than obvious. To make those connections they need to have a wide view of their own specialism, as well as sound knowledge of most other related disciplines.

Consultants also should be honest, so that they tell things as they find them; but they must couple this with sensitivity when necessary. As has already been suggested, in the future advisers will need strong people skills whatever their technical specialism.

Consultancy therefore appears to be an almost impossible job. But most long-time consultants relish their dynamic working environment. They tend to be people who are intolerant of boredom and who need new challenges to stay motivated. Consequently, many consultants have a strongly entrepreneurial attitude and have planned their move into consultancy.

There are also an increasing number of independent 'consultants' who have been forced into this status by redundancy, which is tending to hit middle and senior managers rather more than in the past because of the flattening of management structures. Specialist functions are now being 'outsourced' and the people in them, if they are lucky, are retained on part-time 'consultancy' contracts.

Consultancy places a lot of demands on the individual, and on their family, and requires a particular sort of person. The demands of consultancy make it very difficult for redundant managers and technical specialists to make the switch after a career in, perhaps, a single organisation. Technical skills are not enough: the former manager is likely to lack important skills, such as sales and marketing. They face a steep learning curve with regard to the organisation and practice of consultancy. Without experience in a professional consultancy firm they are likely to make a lot of (expensive) mistakes. Some of these consultants blossom, but many tend not to

69

stick with it. Those people forced into consultancy without understanding the realities of consultancy practice tend to under-price themselves and struggle to make a proper income. Many also over-service clients and thereby compound their problems.

Consultancy approaches

There is a wide range of consultancy approaches. Each specialism has its own ways of working, so it is difficult to be at all specific about adviser's styles. However we can say that there is a move taking place away from the traditional, usually report-based approach, where the adviser comes in, gathers the information, analyses it and produces a report, leaving the client to implement the recommendations. Traditionally there would be little transfer of knowledge, or indeed of the recommendations – the client is essentially on their own from that point. This approach is falling out of favour, but there is a hard core of consultancy firms, not all small, who still favour it, even if they wrap it up in more modern clothing.

The traditional approach is steadily giving way to a more equal partnership between client and consultant. These days consultants tend to work in a much more facilitative way, often in a project team consisting of both consultancy and client staff. Properly handled this ensures a high level of knowledge and skills transfer – in the best projects it is both ways. As before, there may well be reports, findings and recommendations to be documented and shared. The difference is that they should now be fully understood by at least the key members of the client's team.

Consultancy process

The process varies from project to project, but there are common themes to most projects. Variation tends to come with the starting and finishing points of the adviser's involvement, rather than the basic underlying process. Broadly speaking, the steps in a general consultancy project are as follows:

- make proposals to client

- agree terms of reference

- engagement

- problem definition

- information gathering and research

- analysis

- synthesis

- propose solutions

- evaluate solutions against objectives and client capability

- recommend solutions

- plan implementation and determine (outline) budget

- prepare report and make presentations

- review project with client

- disengagement.

All of these steps are discussed in more detail from the client's point of view later in this book.

Accreditation and certification
■   ■   ■

Anyone can call themselves a consultant or many other types of professional adviser; in contrast, there are many professions (such as accountancy, surveying, chartered engineering, etc.) where it is necessary to have particular qualifications and membership of the appropriate professional body. As a general rule, there is little formal regulation of the consultancy industry and, apart from for some of the professions,

71

there are no statutory requirements on who can do what with regard to the provision of *business* advice.

How important then is formal accreditation? Many users of external specialists maintain their own lists of approved specialists. These vary from government agencies, who are subsidising professional support, to large public companies. All have their own parameters for approving such suppliers and monitoring the quality of their interventions.

Even in those professions that do not require formal qualifications there are usually associations and institutes that seek to provide some level of accreditation through their membership grading rules. It must be said that the credibility of such bodies is very varied. However, as a general rule Associate, Affiliate or Licentiate membership grades do not count for a great deal as they are usually the entry point for those entering, or with an interest in, the profession (there are exceptions: fully qualified Chartered Accountants start as Associates – ACA). The one exception is perhaps where someone is moving from one profession to another; for example, an experienced accountant say, ACA (or even FCA) who is moving from finance to management consultancy may be an Associate of the Institute of Management Consultants because they do not (yet) have the three years' experience working *primarily* as a consultant that they need to qualify as a full member. Clearly they may have considerable relevant experience and ability to undertake consultancy projects. So the client often has to look beyond formal qualifications and professional memberships.

The more serious associations require a certain level of qualification combined with a minimum level of appropriate experience (rarely less than three years). Some, such as the Institute of Management, also expect their members to undertake continuing professional development; others such as the Law Society and Institutes of Chartered Accountants, require similar continuing education.

Some brokerage services review each project undertaken

through them and assess the quality of the work. Other consultancy networks also apply their own quality control procedures. For both groups these procedures can vary considerably: they may involve only a superficial scoring of the report against the terms of reference, with little reference to client satisfaction or the achievement of benefits for clients; alternatively, they may comprise a full external audit of the member firm's procedures, quality and adherence to standards on an annual basis, with satisfactory performance required to maintain accreditation. As a rule of thumb, it would appear that the smaller the list of accredited suppliers, the more thorough the validation may be.

In many fields there is no formal approval required, or even requested, by clients. The best certification is satisfied clients, and most experienced advisers rely heavily on their reputation for good work and on referrals from satisfied clients.

73

Executive summary

Consultants and professional advisers can take more than a simple advisory role. For most clients they need to take many roles during the life of the assignment. Technical skills are not sufficient to be an effective consultant – the ability to empathise with the client and to develop a relationship on a personal level is also essential.

Many clients see consultants as people to come in and lift the problems off their shoulders. There is limited scope for doing so because a consultant or adviser should be just that; they are not there to manage the client's business. The responsibility for implementing recommendations and for managing the business must always remain with you, the client and your management team.

Consultancy is largely an unregulated industry; although there are professional associations that do take on some part of that regulatory role, they only have jurisdiction over their members. There are also brokerage services who help clients find advisers, and these services usually apply some measure of quality control over the advisers they accept.

Consultancy approaches vary widely, but there is a general trend towards greater collaboration between client and consultant. This achieves a greater transfer of skills to client staff and promotes a better understanding of any recommendations. This is the way forward for professional advice as clients become more aware of their roles and responsibilities in the process of consultancy.

4
■ ■ ■

Defining the problem or project

The objectives for this chapter are:

- to describe what sort of information is required by most professional advisers;

- to help you to understand the problem or issues you are trying to address;

- to help you to determine the scope and terms of the consultancy project;

- to enable you to do some of the initial investigation work yourself, both to hone your team's skills and to ensure that you are all fully briefed for discussions with the consultant.

Describing the business and the issues
■ ■ ■

Whatever approach you take to a consultancy project you, as the client, will be responsible for the initial description of the business, the markets and regulatory framework in which your organisation operates, and some form of definition of the problem and related issues. You will therefore need to spend time preparing what information you have, or can make, available. The better you can make that information, the less time the consultants will need to spend on their initial review of the organisation. Less time means lower fees!

Doing some of the initial research and documentation yourself will also put you in a better position to define both the terms of reference and the contract for the work. You will be taking control.

There is a basic set of information that is required for most consultancy projects; this then needs to be augmented with project-related information, usually of a more technical nature. First, there should be a brief description of the client organisation, its management and organisational structure, its products or services and its position in the market. It will often be appropriate to include a potted history of the company and how it has got to where it is now. This will give a consultant a feel for the culture of the business – very important if the work is to involve *any* organisational change. Indeed, if the client can provide a concise statement of the organisation's purpose and values then this will be of considerable value.

Once the adviser is appointed, they will probably wish to see the business plan – your formal written document containing clear statements of the business direction and its strategy for achieving the clearly defined corporate objectives. (It need only be a few pages as it should be a working document.) Similarly, if there are other strategy or policy documents that may be relevant, such as documents for marketing or information systems, then they should be made available.

I would wish to see the business plan before setting out on almost any consultancy project – even technical projects. It says so much about the organisation; any consultancy exercise should be geared to meeting the corporate objectives defined in the plan. The business plan is central to setting the terms of reference for almost any project.

Initial analysis
■ ■ ■

Assumptions

There are some implicit assumptions in suggesting that you undertake some of the initial analysis. It might be argued that if you can undertake the initial analysis you probably do not need a consultant. However, we are only talking about an *overview* to identify key values, some of the issues and other general background information. How far you can take the work is a judgement for your management team to make. The consultants will, in any case, want to review this work and satisfy themselves of its validity, although they should not need to repeat the work in its entirety.

Some of the assumptions that are being made when you, as client, are asked to do some initial investigation include the following:

- you know what information is required and where to find it;

- you can express it effectively and share it with the consultant;

- you have the time and sufficient skills to undertake the investigation;

- you can recognise what is germane to the study.

Such assumptions will vary in validity from client to client. A small owner-run business may well have little in the way of the necessary research and communication skills. Even if they have the skills, they may well not have the time and resources needed or ready access to external sources. Whilst, on first examination, one would expect that larger organisations would be able to do such initial analysis and would have the skills, resources and access, it is not necessarily so. Many large bodies have lost much of their middle management and technical departments have been 'outsourced'. As a result both the resources and the necessary expertise are no longer available within the organisation – that is often why they are using external advisers in the first place. Even so, it is still desirable that the client's staff do some of the initial preparatory work; if only to make themselves more knowledgeable customers and to gain personal credibility with the consultant. As has already been stressed several times, a good consultancy relationship depends on mutual trust and respect. Both parties need to establish their capabilities with the other.

78

Information needed

There are three broad types of information required to support any review or analysis work:

- current business activity

- internal environment

- general external environment.

These are described below.

Current business activity

The organisation's background
This simply comprises a potted recent history together with any long-term aspects that may influence the work.

√ **Finance**
Inevitably on most projects there is a financial dimension, if

only as a constraint on affordable solutions. You have not only to be able to afford the advice but also to be able to pay for the implementation of recommendations. You should undertake a cost–benefit analysis as a precursor to any investment and purchasing consultancy should be regarded as an investment.

A starting point will always be the statutory accounts, but if there are management accounts these should be made available if required. The management accounts can be particularly illuminating, not just because of the figures, but also through their thoroughness, timeliness and reliability.

Costing and pricing information is also often needed and, in any case, ought to be available, as should budget details and performance against budget.

Customers

Why do others use or buy from the client organisation? What is the typical profile of customers (wholesaler or retailer, large or small, local or international etc.)? Thought needs to be given to what customers need and expect from you as a supplier – it may well be more than simply your product. What about delivery, technical or other supporting information, long-term support or guidance on the use of your products?

79

Consultant's Casebook

REORGANISING A SALES FUNCTION

A client was seeking to gain control of his sales function and to reduce costs. His sales team consisted of networked agents – some were employed, others were freelance on a commission only basis. The client was proposing to move to a centralised telesales operation supported by a new computer system – he hoped to reduce the time between order and delivery and to make savings on his stock-holding.

We talked to customers to find out what they needed to help us specify the requirements for the new computer software and to identify the new staffing and training requirements. As we talked

▶

▶

it became clear that the client was missing a vital point – the customers placed very high value on the regular, personal contact. Part of the service the customers, who effectively worked alone, were buying was a regular fortnightly or monthly meeting with a friendly face. If they lost that, the company would lose many of their customers to the competition, who were cheaper but did not offer the same personal service.

The result was that the customer retained the local agents but gave them portable computers which allowed them to place their orders electronically at the end of the day. At the same time as sending in their orders the agents were sent their performance figures, details of new enquiries, sales promotions information, new product information and were prompted as to which customers needed to be contacted.

Sales increased, margins were maintained and in some cases they improved.

Market

There needs to be a review of the market in which the business operates and the degree of regulation it is subject to. This will include the competitive position of the company, the size of the potential market, the degree of globalisation and details of the main competitors and their position in the market.

Products

There must be review of the products in relation to the market, their history and, if known, their relative market share. Useful information for many consultancy projects is the extent to which each product uses resources and contributes to the organisation's income and profit.

Technology

A review of technology should cover not only the technology used by the client but also that used by its competitors and any future changes that may be foreseen. This latter point may include internal development, external technology change and substitute technologies that may be coming to fruition.

An example of a substitute technology was the emergence of the discrete transistor, which replaced thermionic valves and which in turn has been overtaken, to a large extent, first by analogue integrated circuits and, more recently, digital electronic devices. Even now laboratories are working on the next step which is the replacement of semiconductor computer 'chips' with optical or even biological devices.

Suppliers
This should cover the main suppliers, including relationships, pricing strategies and the competition for the client's custom.

Business structure (group, subsidiaries, etc.)
There should be a description of the way the business is structured, both as a corporate entity and within each body, in terms of departmental or functional responsibilities. Included with this information should be the staff, budgets and their roles within the organisation.

Include in this section a brief résumé on each of the key people and give the consultant the opportunity to review personnel files. After all, any organisation is only a collection of people and processes – the consultant needs to understand both.

General external environment

Statutory and regulatory framework
If the organisation operates within a regulatory or statutory regime then this must be explained, especially if the consultants being used are not industry specialists. Those aspects of the regulations that apply to the client should be available, with background explanation to ensure that there is a common interpretation.

Planning and local regulations
The business may be influenced by local planning laws, and the nature of the activities at particular sites may be con-

strained by zoning or noise regulations. There may also be other local policy issues which the client has to respect if they are to maintain good relations with the local authorities. These should all be available to the consultant, if needed, with appropriate explanation and clarification as necessary.

Public perception
Increasingly all organisations have to consider how the wider population, not just their customers, see them. Again, it is an aspect of which any adviser should be aware, because many changes, including internal ones, expressed in the wrong way, can send an undesirable message to the wider community.

Political environment

Most organisations are influenced by the political climate, but some, such as government agencies and the public sector, are directly influenced by a change of political direction at national, or indeed local, level. Advisers need to be sensitive to such issues and perhaps to be made aware of what a possible incoming government is saying in relation to the client's sphere of operations. The client's strategies, and therefore the consultant's advice, will have to take account of the uncertainty and to incorporate plans that can accommodate whatever happens.

Internal environment

Shared purpose and values

Whether formally documented or not, each organisation has a culture of its own. The extent to which there is a shared view of where the business is going and how it should get there is a different matter. Ideally the client needs to make advisers aware of both the formal and informal views. It may be that the 'party line' is detailed in the business plan or strategic direction documents.

Management structure
Although organisational structure has been discussed in relation to current business activity, the management struc-

ture and process may not be the same. Often they are supposed to be, but in practice there are differences. To the extent that these are understood, they should be available to the consultant.

Planning processes

A logical follow-on to management structure is how the business does its planning. This will include everything from the annual budget-setting process to defining the strategic direction and business planning. To what extent are staff encouraged and enabled to contribute to the planning? Apart from saying a lot about the organisation, it is essential for the external adviser to understand this as they will not want to cause friction by inadvertently diverging from existing practice. The consultants may well use different processes and people, but this should be agreed with the client in the light of current practice.

83

As well as routine planning, the consultant will need to understand the decision process for *ad hoc* decisions with regard to investment, etc. Their recommendations may need to be fed into that process for establishing a possible budget for implementation.

Technology

Depending on the nature of the consultancy work, the consultant may want to know something about the use of technology in almost any area. This will include, amongst others:

- products

- production (services or manufacturing)

- support services, information systems, design, research, etc.

As the nature of information required will be very variable it may simply be that the consultant needs to be given a quick overview of the technology in use, and to be supported by guidance on who to speak to for detailed information.

Communication

Closely linked with both management structure and planning process, communication methods need to be understood by any adviser. They need to understand how, when and where their project will be discussed so that they can make themselves available to all interested parties and ensure that the purpose of their work is not misrepresented or simply misunderstood.

Internal politics

To some extent internal politics will be covered by the culture of the organisation. However, as was discussed with regard to consultants' fears in Chapter 2, the consultant should be made aware of any power struggles or other tensions in the organisation. They will find them in any case, but they will be more effective and less likely to make mistakes if they are forewarned.

As an aside, this information should still be prepared if the project is being undertaken internally – it helps to prevent the project team from making rash or inappropriate assumptions.

Doing it yourself
■ ■ ■

As part of the relationship with the external adviser you, the client, are seeking to develop your own skills through knowledge and skills transfer from the consultant. But first you need to polish your existing skills. The initial analysis is an ideal opportunity to do so and to decide where your limits as an organisation are.

There are several basic techniques that you may well have met before and that you can easily undertake with a little guidance. The consultant may well use some of them with you as part of the project, but that will not mean that the work you have done yourself is wasted. In the first instance you will have learned from the exercise (if only how difficult it is to do well!) and you will have used your findings to set the terms and scope of the project for the consultant. The consultant will also be building on your work and will be seeking other or additional information

Problem definition

The problem definition process starts by listing the symptoms, whilst avoiding jumping to conclusions or concentrating on imagined causes. The aim is to start with what we know, not with guesses.

The next step is to quantify the problem, or at least to collate any factual measures or indicators that may be related to or influenced by the symptoms. At this stage you are not trying to tie the symptoms and measures together. You are simply fact finding. The measures will very much depend on the nature of the problem: cash flow problems will (probably) need different measures from those you need when you are investigating why you are having so much downtime with your computer system. The appropriate measures are not always the obvious ones, as the case study below illustrates.

85

Consultant's Casebook

EXPECT THE UNEXPECTED

A colleague and I were called in to a client because they were having cash flow problems and were not achieving the sales figures that they had anticipated. They had been on target, but in the last few periods performance had declined significantly.

Our brief was to help to define the problem and then, if necessary, to help select suitable specialist advisers to resolve it. So my accountant colleague looked at the numbers whilst I examined the procedures. The procedures seemed slick enough: it was a telesales operation taking orders by telephone and logging them straight onto the computer. Calls were being answered within two rings, as shown by sampling performance,

▶

▶

and most resulted in an order being placed; everyone seemed to be working as fast as the computer allowed.

My colleague was able to confirm that there had been a quite steep fall in sales over a two-month period around the year end, and that it had flattened at the new level about ten per cent below expectation. Average order value was unchanged, so that was not the problem. We had quantification of the problem but no real solution. The client knew from discussions with other companies and his suppliers that the market as a whole had not collapsed – the demand was still there.

We then pulled several of the directors into a brainstorming session to try to identify as many changes as possible that had happened during the last year – we simply wanted all the facts we could get our hands on. It turned out that they had upgraded their computer system at the year end. They had not replaced it, the new software should have been a routine new release, but it had been troublesome and they had had many problems which had taken the system out of operation. These had been quickly resolved over a two-month period and the system had been trouble-free ever since, so they had discounted it as the cause. It was the only anomaly that we could spot, so we investigated further.

We discovered that calls were taking slightly longer to handle, but this had not been detected because of the problems at the changeover. By the time the system had settled down the operators had lost their feel for the speed of the old version. Although there had been some minor comments that it was slower, these were considered to be a backlash from the earlier problems.

Because calls were taking slightly longer, more customers were failing to get through and inevitably they did not all try again when the telephone lines were quieter. We did some calculations and discovered that, because they were close to capacity on their lines, they were getting about a fifteen per cent increase in engaged calls, most of whom were not coming back at other times; hence the ten per cent drop in sales.

The client increased the number of lines and operators and

recovered most of the lost sales in the first full month. In time they found that they actually increased sales because it had become much easier to place an order!

In this case it would have been easy to have assumed that the promotion approach was wrong and then spent a lot on extra advertising. Do not jump to conclusions: collect data and then analyse it, make the connection, then come to possible causes and test them explicitly. Once there is no doubt, then you can determine the solution and of course implement it. Easy really!

Appropriate measures may be budgets or anticipated sales, they may be actual sales performance by product or anything else that is measured in relation to the organisation's performance. They may even be measures relating to competitors' performance – how have their sales changed during the period?

The next step is to collect any other known facts with all supporting evidence. Again facts, not supposition. These could be anything from the date a senior manager left to economic or industrial trends outside the organisation. For instance, in hospitals there tends to be less elective surgery done during the winter. We would need to know about that trend, and other seasonal trends, to identify that because there are more patients with breathing and related problems there is greater demand for emergency medical (as opposed to surgical) beds during those months. As a result, surgeons do not have the beds available to handle as many non-emergency patients as during the summer.

It will now become possible to use this information to compare performance against that of competitors, or against expectations. From that we can start to measure the deficiency. At this stage of the analysis we can begin to get some sort of feel for the possible causes, so we must resist the temptation to jump to conclusions.

All problem-solving hinges on having a belief that a solution is possible. With most business problems, especially if the problem is caught early, there will be a satisfactory solution.

SWOT or COST

The analysis approaches SWOT and COST are essentially the same. They differ in emphasis. Both consider the capabilities and influences on an organisation (they are quite useful too for analysing and planning your own career) under four headings:

SWOT   Strengths, Weakness, Opportunities and Threats

COST   Concerns, Opportunities, Strengths and Threats

Most managers will be familiar with SWOT at least, so I will just cover the main differences in content and approach between the two techniques. Like Tom Lambert, who originated it in *High Income Consulting*, I personally prefer COST as I find it has a rather more positive emphasis. I would suggest you use the one with which you are most comfortable. Both techniques can be used by individuals, but they are most effective when undertaken by a smallish group of people (around six) who trust each other and who can therefore be completely open with each other. If working in a group you will need to use a variety of techniques that might include, amongst many others:

- brainstorming
- mind-mapping
- internal staff surveys (both confidential and open)
- quality circles
- customer reviews and surveys
- supplier reviews and surveys
- staff appraisals.

Concerns

One first considers those issues and practices that give concern. They might be your organisation's skills base, cash position, market position or whatever. It does not matter how trivial a concern may seem, it should be included as long as it is relevant to the customer and affects your product or service. Do not at this stage worry about what, or even whether, anything can be done about it. Just list all those that can be supported by hard evidence.

Opportunities

Next consider the opportunities within your organisation for improvement or positive change, and outside your organisation in the market place. Think what opportunities you might have by using your skills, technology, contacts, knowledge, etc. Again, however minor, list them all initially. With the likely wide readership of this book a definitive list of what constitutes a relevant opportunity is not possible. Some opportunities that spring to mind include:

89

- legislative changes

- market improvements

- a competitor pulling out of the market

- demographic changes, e.g. more over-60s

and many, many more.

From that list you can examine each option in more detail, determine those that can be exploited and plan your response to make the most of them.

Strengths

Next, be really aggressive in looking for your strengths both in the general sense and in relation to addressing your concerns and responding to opportunities. Be positive and again list everything, however modest. I have done this with many dispirited groups and, however poorly they have been told they are doing, they always have strengths and always have some real achievements.

Some strengths will be unique to you as an organisation or department. Does the strength matter to your customer? If it does and nobody else is offering it, then you have found part of your unique edge over the competition.

Threats

You should now consider the threats that might prevent you responding to opportunities or addressing your concerns. Again, be as comprehensive as you can because they will provide a basis for your risk assessment and contingency planning. If you are aware that something could get in the way, then it will not come as a surprise as you will be watching for the early signs. You will need to define what those signs might be.

Bear in mind that as you start measuring things matters appear to get worse – people become more skilled at spotting problems. To avoid demotivation use positive ('we got it right') measures such as percentage of deliveries on time (rather than how many are late) or percentage attendance (rather than absenteeism).

This is the first step of many planning processes, strategic or operational, and normally you would take these through to a solution and a detailed plan with measurable objectives. However, here we are talking about preparing the ground for a consultant by identifying the issues and challenges so that you can decide on the nature of the project brief. If you wish to take them further yourself, then I suggest you read some of the books listed in Appendix B which have room to do more justice to the planning process.

Flowcharting

For many projects we need to understand the steps that are happening and the decisions being taken along the way. A simple method is flowcharting, and there are many computer software tools to assist with drawing pretty diagrams. The important thing is usually to get an overview of the big picture; for this a simple hand-drawn chart is good enough. After all, you are seeking to make changes and improve the way things are done, so the chart depicting the status quo is a working document rather than a finished presentation documentation.

As well as the flows of a business process I would recommend that you also look at where and how information is recorded. The informal aspects of the process tend to be the important ones – they are the ones that people actually use. Some years ago I did some work for a hospital department and one of the keys to one speciality was a notebook that the consultant (a surgeon) carried in his white coat – it contained a list of everything he had asked anyone to do. His staff knew that if he had delegated something to them they had better do it because he would not forget it even if they did. The operations director mentioned elsewhere uses a pocket electronic organiser for the same purpose, and with the same results.

91

Consultant's Casebook

WASTING EFFORT

I ran an exercise for a large mental health hospital which we called a 'paperchase'. We were tracking the flow of patient details from initial referral through the patient's treatment to eventual discharge or death (it was a long-stay hospital and many patients were there for the last few years of their lives).

There were supposed to be well-defined procedures in operation and there was some support for the process from the computer based systems. But the expectation and the reality were very different! To be fair to the client, that was what they suspected and why we were undertaking the exercise.

There were places where the patient's name and address were recorded seven or eight times. Almost every person working in administration had their own index to the patient's record, as did many of the clinical staff; this despite the details being supposedly held on shared computer systems.

This was in a hospital where they were particularly concerned about confidentiality. Many of the patients would not want

▶

▶

> anyone to know that they were being treated there – there is still a stigma attached to mental illness by many people. With all those manual and individual personal computer databases, under little control, how could confidentiality be expected, let alone guaranteed? It also raised serious issues with regard to their Data Protection Act compliance and other matters. The client acted very quickly to redesign completely the way they handled this process. Simple flowcharting was very illuminating.

Systems analysis

Decomposition is a systems approach to analysis. A system consists of inputs to a process which produces outputs. Most systems can therefore be broken down into progressively smaller sub-systems. The organisation as a whole can be regarded as a system which can then be decomposed into more manageable sub-systems.

Essentially there are three elements to systems analysis:

- inputs – what goes into the system, orders, raw materials, money;
- process – what is done to the inputs;
- outputs – what comes out of the system as a result of the process acting on the inputs.

First, consider the high-level corporate system and document what goes in, what comes out and what has happened to it in between. It should all fit onto a single piece of paper.

Then move down a level and consider the sub-systems that make up the whole. Repeat the documentation of inputs, outputs and processes at this level. Continue breaking down the systems until they are small enough to handle as an entity. To ensure completeness, the diagrams or other forms of documentation should obey two rules:

- all outputs must be required and must go somewhere;
- all inputs must be available.

There are a variety of formal techniques for structured systems analysis such as SSADM (Structured Systems Analysis and Design Method) and CORE (Controlled Requirements Expression). These have a substantial literature of their own and it would be inappropriate even to start detailing them here. Devise your own approach to documentation. After all it is intended to support the consultant, and both what has been done and how it was performed will give the consultant a valuable insight into the organisation and its capabilities.

Departmental purpose analysis

This is a useful tool which follows on logically from flowcharting or systems analysis as it requires an understanding of both the processes and the input/output analysis. It helps departments, or logical workgroups, to align their objectives to the corporate objectives. It also clarifies relationships with suppliers and customers and allows performance measures to be established. Although I talk in terms of departments, they may not necessarily be the functional departments currently in use – they should be groupings aligned to meeting customer needs, not administrative needs. Such groupings will be based on consideration of the systems analysis and the departmental purpose itself.

The analysis requires three sets of questions to be answered and the associated performance quantified:

Are we doing the right things?

- What is the purpose of the department?

- Who are our customers (both internal and external)?

- Who are our suppliers (both internal and external)?

- What do our customers need from us?

- Where are we not meeting those customer needs?

- Why do we do this task or activity?

- Why do we do those things that give no value to the customer?

Are we doing things right?

- Which is our priority issue (from above)?

- What are the real causes of the problem?

- What are the best suppliers achieving in this area? What constitutes 'world class'?

- What is the best solution to that problem?

- Does the solution eliminate the problem to the customers' satisfaction?

- Will the solution prevent reoccurrence?

- What is the next priority issue?

Are we always looking for improvements?

- Once we have addressed the priority problems and are satisfying customers, what can we do to improve our efficiency and effectiveness?

- What are the priority areas for improvement?

Quality functional deployment

This is an approach to process design that combines analysis of inputs and outputs, causes and effects, problem-solving, etc. to identify where best to invest time, money and effort.

The basic approach is quite simple:

1 Brainstorm or mind-map to identify both the requirements and how they can be met.

2 Establish the strength of relationships between 'what' can be done and 'how' it can be done. This can then be analysed by using pie-charts, cause and effect diagrams and matrix analysis as below.

	How			
What	How-1	How-2	How-3	...
What–1	L		M	
What–2	H	H	L	
What–3	L	L		
...				
Score:	11	10	4	

H=very strong relationship (rating=9)
M=strong relationship (rating=3)
L=weak relationship (rating=1)

The scores then provide a focus for appropriate action – use the 80:20 rule to decide where the effort will be best used. It will be a matter of judgement as to whether it can be undertaken in-house or whether it provides the basis of the problem definition for a consultancy project.

Consequence analysis

A technique that I have found useful is consequence analysis. It is simple, but it can show inter-dependencies that would not at first sight seem obvious.

Quite simply, one lists actions, problems or issues in any order, using just one-line descriptions. One then considers which follow on as a consequence of another. These may be circular in that A leads on to B which leads to A. They may be two-way, where A is a consequence of B and A is a consequence of B. By drawing this as a diagram, one can see points that are a focus of many events and therefore that will pay further analysis.

I developed my approach from Edward de Bono's ' flowscapes' in his book, *Water Logic*. At this stage my own interpretation of his techniques and my applications are still relatively crude, as I am still developing them. It is one of several tools I use for putting my own thoughts in order. I would suggest that if you are interested in the idea you go back to the source and develop your own approach from de Bono's work.

Numerical analysis

Wherever possible one should get at the hard facts and quantify the issues. Some form of numerical analysis will be needed on almost any project to form the basis for further qualitative investigation. The two approaches will then have to be brought back together again to quantify the likely improvement, costs, etc. for the proposed solutions.

So a client can help a consultant by pulling relevant numerical data together. Although I have called this section *Numerical Analysis*, it is probably rather more about data collection. You are collecting data and undertaking any analysis in preparation for using an external adviser; if you are not careful you may hide important information if you get your analysis wrong, so ensure that you also provide the raw data.

The sort of quantification and analysis that might be useful could include:

- sales and costs by product;

- number of telephone calls and their average duration;

- population of area served by proposed sewage works;

- investment by project;

the list is endless.

You will need to discuss what information would be useful with prospective consultants, or in more detail with your selected adviser.

Talk to the consultant about what preparation you can do

Ask the consultant what preparatory work you can undertake that will help them when they get on-site. The consultant should be happy to give you guidance as to what analysis you could do before they start. Most advisers will give general advice at the initial contact stage when you are trying to establish your short list. This will only be a guide, as you cannot expect free detailed advice, but it will allow you to get started. More importantly it means you will be better able to brief the incoming consultant – remember that good consultancy needs a good client.

If there is to be a gap between commissioning the consultant and the start of the project, then your new adviser will be able, and willing, to give you more specific advice on what internal analysis could be done to help them to make a flying start.

Consultant's tip

Traditional techniques for measuring productivity require people with clipboards and stopwatches, or timesheets and computer analysis. However, there is a quick and easy way for getting a **feel** for the productivity of a group of staff when they are based in one place.

When you walk into an office count the number of people working and divide it by the number of people in the office. Repeat this occasionally (not every five minutes!) and average the results over a period of time. The figure you get will tend towards the same figure achieved by more rigorous methods. This will give a useful guide to activity, but it does not measure anything about the effectiveness of the work being done.

In a normal, busy administrative office the guideline productivity figure produced in this way would be around 80–85%.

Project definition

■ ■ ■

Definition of the project or problem is central to achieving success. Without effective definition of the objectives it will not be possible to measure whether success has been achieved! Whilst the prospective client has to define the problem in the first instance, it is the responsibility of the client and consultant together to determine the objectives for the work. Here they are particularly concerned with the need for the client to provide enough information for the consultant to assess what is involved in the project, without effectively giving the consultant complete freedom to set their own terms.

> ### Consultant's tip
>
> *If you do not understand the problem enough to be able to assess what professional support you need, then why not make the definition of the problem a small project in its own right? It is preferable to doing nothing or to giving a firm of advisers a completely free hand.*
>
> *This sort of project can either be undertaken by a small team internally or by a generalist consultant who could help you gain sufficient understanding to specify the problem for the main project. If you use external support the work should only require a few days of the consultant's time – often it is sufficient to use the consultant to facilitate a one-day workshop for the senior management team and others (remember senior management do not have a monopoly on wisdom or perception). Please note, whatever the piece of work required it must have* full and unequivocal *support from the top of the organisation.*

Project phases

As a general guide, most projects are based on a structure similar to the following:

- project definition

- information gathering/research

- analysis and synthesis

- recommendations

- implementation

- final evaluation

- disengagement.

The structure may vary quite considerably with regard to the detail and the way in which it is undertaken. However, it will be underpinned by the above steps.

Project objectives

99

The project objectives should be stated in terms of business benefits, and those benefits should support the achievement of the corporate objectives in the business plan. Achievement of the objectives should therefore be in no doubt because you have defined them in unambiguous terms. Like all objectives, they should be stated in such a way that they are SMART:

- **S**pecific – precise with no doubt as to what has to be delivered, and, ideally, what this means in terms of business objectives.

- **M**easurable – put numbers to the objectives even if it is 100%. An objective ought to be measured in terms of the measures already in place for the corporate objectives.

- **A**chievable.

- **R**ealistic – they must be possible.

- **T**imed – they should have a date by which they should be achieved.

If the objectives and benefits are clear then the adviser and the client both know when the work has been completed – and the project should not be able to creep if any reasonable management discipline is in place. The client and consultant will also know how successful they have been, because they will be able to score their performance against the measures that were agreed before the work started.

Boundaries/ scope of the project

You need to keep the project manageable, so you will have to put boundaries on it. However, this can be awkward with the increasingly cross-functional nature of business advice. For example, what initially looks like a marketing issue can easily broaden to include finance, production, information systems, human resources and almost any other function. So restricting the scope on a functional basis is likely to put false and inappropriate constraints on the solutions. This could easily result in the full benefits not being fully realised. You need to find another way of keeping the project focused and within bounds.

I would argue that you should already have what is needed in the form of the project objectives. If you make the objectives clear, then any action taken, be it investigation, analysis or implementation, has to be demonstrably directed towards achieving the agreed project objectives. Otherwise it is outside the terms of reference and should not form part of the project.

Skills needed/ available

You need to make an assessment of the type of skills that the project will require. This will be on the basis of what has been established about the nature and scope of the work. The next step is to decide whether resources with appropriate competencies are available in-house, and whether they can be released to undertake the proposed project. Bear in mind that the project plan might well slip, and the consultant may have to stay longer then originally requested. It would be very wasteful to pull a key member of the project team out during the critical final stages of a project: it would seriously affect the project timetable if someone new had to be brought in, as they would need time to assimilate all the work that had been done.

By this point you should have a reasonably clear view of what your organisation can do itself and what support it will need from outside advisers. You can now move on to the next step.

Budget

All projects should have a pre-defined budget based on a realistic assessment of all the costs to be incurred as a result of undertaking the work. As little as possible should be covered by general overheads, as they will be nobody's responsibility and will usually not be effectively managed. The project's costs should therefore stand completely alone and be the responsibility of the client's project manager.

101

Consultant's tip

Make large projects manageable by breaking them up into a several smaller projects. The first project will probably be an overall review to set the scope and terms of reference for the subsequent projects. This approach will also allow the use, with care, of different specialist firms for the sub-projects, so long as you can do so without creating artificial functional distinctions between the different elements of the work.

A few words of warning. As discussed earlier, one has to plan such multiple projects carefully to avoid losing sight of the bigger picture – they need very careful co-ordination and make enormous demands on the project team with overall responsibility. Also one needs to be very careful with the timing of the elements to avoid initiative overload on groups and individuals – they need time to assimilate change before moving on to the next step.

Executive summary

Every project requiring investment should start by defining its purpose and what it is to achieve. Investment in professional advice is no different. You need a clear description of the organisation, its business, how it is structured, its technology and how it sees itself.

There are several ways in which a client can prepare themselves so that they can both select the right consultant and brief them properly when they have done so. It is important that the client does some initial analysis so that they understand as much as possible of the problem and the state of their own organisation. By being prepared the client can also reduce the need for the consultant to do the basic analysis, and thereby minimise the fees.

It is important that the client only collects the facts and does not prejudge the solutions. If they start to guess at causes their briefing will tend to steer advisers in that direction and, as I have illustrated, the reasons for the problem may not lend themselves to simple judgements. If you are going to use consultants leave the analysis to them and to your project team.

The client has to set boundaries to the assignment so that it can be managed. Similarly, the objectives should be clearly defined and measurable. There is a balance to be drawn between room for creativity and focus on the important issues – the client has to be clear about where this balance point lies, so that the terms of reference can be agreed.

Checklist

Ask yourself if you have described the business and the issues:

1 Are the essential documents available: business plan, management accounts, last audited accounts?

2 Have we described the current state of business, markets, products, staff, technology?

3 Have we a sufficiently detailed description of the external environment in which the organisation operates? What regulations apply? What is our public face?

4 Is there a clear statement about the internal environment of the organisation? Does this cover structure, vision and values, culture, trust and other communication and management issues?

5 Have we done some initial analysis to identify the issues?

6 Have we described the problem only in terms of symptoms and known facts rather than as guesses as to the cause?

7 Have we set appropriate boundaries to the project – not in terms of function or department but in terms of the business process to be investigated?

8 Have we SMART objectives for the project? Do they relate directly to SMART corporate objectives in the business plan? Are they really measurable?

9 Have we determined a budget for the assignment – even if only as an initial estimate?

10 Have we really told it how it is, warts and all?

5

■ ■ ■

Selecting a consultant

The objectives of this chapter are as follows:

- to provide a structured selection process for choosing profes- sional advisers;

- to show you how to identify an initial list of potential consult- ants;

- to give you some tools for use in reducing the initial list to a manageable short list;

- to set out a formal process for inviting bids and for their subse- quent evaluation.

This chapter also sets out to provide assistance with the particu- lar issues facing the not-for-profit sector including public-sector organisations, charities, voluntary organisations, local and cen- tral government and their agencies.

Competitive tendering
■ ■ ■

Increasingly, major organisations are using competitive tendering to select their professional advisers, regardless of whether these are auditors, merchant banks, management consultants, or technical specialists such as engineers and information technologists. This approach is not new, especially within the 'creative' professions such as advertising agents and designers, but it is now increasingly being used for the traditional professions, such as lawyers and accountants.

It has long been common practice in the public sector for all such work to be tendered, because of the need to have auditable purchasing practices and to be seen to be even-handed in approach. The growing importance of corporate governance has also been a driver for change in major commercial organisations, and there have also been cost pressures, increased competition and a wider range of options for addressing each business need. Clients want to make the most of such benefits and see tendering as a way of doing so.

The thinking behind competitive tendering is that it provides wide choice, competitive fees and encourages innovation by advisers. It must be said that it is also used as a weapon against existing advisers, forcing them to keep their quality up and their fees down.

However, there is a downside in that competitive tendering can be costly and slow. Done properly, it is time-consuming and makes particularly heavy demands on senior staff. Done badly, it can be worse than the more traditional methods, which relied on knowing people who could do the job, albeit at a price.

Is it really necessary to use competitive tendering for all pro-jects? One has to be clear about the objectives. If the reason is to drive an existing adviser's fees down or to address other problems, then there are more appropriate means. Frank dis-cussion between a senior representative of both client and consultancy is more likely to bear fruit; the threat of going out to tender can always be held in reserve and used as an implicit threat. That, of course, assumes that we are essen-tially happy with the incumbent firm, and, indeed, that there is someone in place.

Most organisations of any size will have professional advisers in place for audit and so on, but for one-off projects they will need to choose a suitable firm. Even then, if there is a favoured firm (even when changing an existing adviser), then it might be more cost-effective to negotiate directly. However, I would still suggest that the preferred adviser should be required to produce a proposal as a basis for negotiation. To prepare a proposal they will need similar documents from the client that set out the background and the nature of the pro-posed work. These will be similar to those used for competi-tive tendering, so much of the same process can be adopted with some simplification and less formality. There is then still the option of easily switching to a full competitive tendering process if negotiations stumble; many of the necessary ele-ments will already be in place.

107

All that said and done, competitive tendering, or 'beauty parades' as they are known in some circles, are a good test for the competing bidders. They demonstrate whether a firm can innovate or be creative under pressure. Each firm will have only one chance to get it right, so will need good information from the client and the opportunity to check their under-standing and to resolve any questions they may have. A beauty parade should not just be about the lowest fees, but also about who has the best ideas, most appreciation of the issues and, perhaps above all, who is the best cultural fit with the client.

Choosing the right number of bidders

Probably the biggest and most common mistake made by clients when selecting suppliers, not just advisers, is that of inviting too many to bid and, even worse, including too many on the final short list of firms asked to give presentations. My own experience is that inviting too many bidders is a particularly common mistake in the public sector. It is often due to the client underestimating the amount of work involved for the bidder in preparing a proposal, and the amount of time needed for the client to evaluate the responses properly.

There seems to be a common misapprehension that increasing the number of bidders will increase the choice. This is not usually the case. I have assisted on such bids: most of the bidders can be ruled out easily, and most of the remaining ones would have been included on the short list anyway. All it does is add substantial additional work in the process which could have been avoided with a little more homework. So make sure that the short list are really competing for the work and not just making up numbers to give spurious credibility to the process.

A typical proposal in response to an invitation to tender will cost the bidder something like 5 – 20% of the fee. Someone has to bear that cost and, at the end of the day, it has to be clients. Another point to bear in mind is that if there are too many bidders (and you should be prepared to divulge the number, if not the names, of those asked to bid) some firms, possibly strongly favoured ones, will not bid. Because of the cost and the risk with so many competitors it can, on balance, be deemed not to be cost-effective to bid. I have certainly declined to bid on that basis when working for both small and large consultancy firms.

Selection process

■ ■ ■

The selection process is essentially the same whatever the

size or nature of the work being commissioned. There will be short cuts for smaller projects and some additional steps where European Union rules apply but these do not affect the underlying process. The basic steps in the selection process are as follows:

■ identify and describe the essential problem;

■ appoint selection committee;

■ create a long list of possible suppliers;

■ define the problem in more detail;

■ narrow the possible suppliers down to a short list;

■ prepare invitation to tender documents;

■ prepare evaluation criteria;

■ decide on evaluation approach;

■ organise query resolution procedure for bidders;

■ send out tender documents with a clear deadline;

■ resolve queries/meet bidders;

■ receive proposals;

■ evaluate proposals against predefined evaluation criteria;

■ resolve queries;

■ advise short list of suppliers chosen to make presentations;

■ organise presentation facilities;

■ prepare questions/format of presentation;

■ prepare evaluation criteria for presentation;

■ presentations;

■ evaluate presentations;

■ select supplier;

- negotiate final terms of contract/terms of reference;

- place contract with chosen adviser;

- advise the unsuccessful bidders;

- debrief unsuccessful bidders – if requested;

- arrange initial planning meeting with selected adviser.

It is important to follow a consistent logical process and not to cut corners. The steps you have predefined for your selection should be such that it is auditable in respect of value for money and equity. This auditability is essential for public sector procurement of any product or service, and it is good practice for anyone. Short cuts may result in the wrong consultants undertaking the wrong project.

Documentation

Finally, whatever approach you adopt it should be properly documented so that there is no confusion on anyone's part about what has been agreed. This should start with the remit of the selection committee and should include all discussion with consultants and prospective consultants. If one is to be able to demonstrate that the bid process has been above board, one will have to be able to show that any given bidder was excluded for clear reasons. As will be seen later, documentation will also be important for debriefing unsuccessful bidders.

Most of the time, a handwritten contemporaneous note of a telephone conversation or meeting in the file will suffice. Significant matters, and all decisions, especially in the later stages of detailed negotiation, should be confirmed in a letter or in formal minutes. All should be filed as part of the procurement documentation.

This is not simply bureaucracy. Such notes are important to the negotiation of terms and may ultimately be incorporated in the final contract and terms of reference. For public-sector procurement, such notes could, in extreme circumstances, have to be produced in court to justify why a particular supplier was chosen or another excluded. Unsuccessful bidders can, under EU/GATT regulations, challenge the award of a contract if they believe that the process has not complied with the rules.

Selection committee

All through the process of selecting consultants, decisions will need to be made. Therefore the selection committee who will have responsibility for selecting the consultants should be appointed at the earliest opportunity. They should have clear terms of reference and the committee should have a limited life. But, most importantly, they should have full authority to make the selection, with the possible exception of a need to seek board ratification of the appointment. It may therefore be appropriate for the selection committee to be chaired by a Director or senior manager, depending on the size, scope and nature of the proposed work.

111

The selection committee should have a suitable mix of skills and representation. Clearly it should have specialist skills to allow it to prepare the technical parts of the invitation to tender documents and subsequently to assess the technical competence of the bidders. It should consist of those who will have to work most closely with the consultant, and there should also be representatives from other relevant interests.

As we have already recognised, people issues are crucial to most change programmes and so someone with human resource management skills may be useful. Also, the users or those who will be affected by the recommendations of the advisers may need some form of representation.

At all costs avoid making the committee too large – it reduces efficiency rather more than improving the quality of decisions. Bear in mind that the committee can seek advice from elsewhere within the organisation should it be needed. Also consider the cost of pulling a large group away from their other work. For the majority of projects a small committee of no more than five should suffice, and for most selections three should be sufficient.

Thought should be given to whether the selection team should be the project team once the consultant is in harness. I would strongly suggest that they should; that way they have to make their decision work. This should be made clear at the outset in the remit that the group is given. Additional people may need to be added to the group to form the project team depending on the skills required and the organisation of the project.

Timetable and diaries

At the first meeting the committee should agree the timetable for the bid so that everyone can put aside the appropriate dates. Apart from any routine meetings during the development of the invitation documents, the key dates are as follows:

- to agree final short list of bidders;
- closing date for proposals – may not require time from the committee but they may have to set time aside to read proposals before the evaluation meeting;
- opening date for tenders or evaluation meeting;
- for presentations – should usually all be on one day (or two consecutive days at most);
- evaluation date for presentations – if not the same date as the presentations;
- dates for negotiations with favoured supplier up to and including award of contracts;
- for debriefing meeting for unsuccessful bidders;
- date for planning with appointed advisers.

Sharing information

If different people from the selection committee are going to meet prospective advisers at different times, there has to be an agreed procedure for sharing information and impressions amongst all committee members.

At each of the three main stages there will be slightly different requirements. At the initial stage of identifying a long list of possible firms the information is a mixture of background, hard quantitative details (turnover, number of consultants etc.) and personal judgements. The background, where it originates verbally in meetings or over the telephone, should be recorded in a note made at the time. Copies should be circulated to each member of the team. Where there are brochures and other documents these should either be circulated or, probably more conveniently, placed in a central location – at the committee chairperson's office perhaps. In that case only a note of new material that has been filed will need to be advised to other team members.

113

Personal impressions and judgements should be recorded and shared as for notes of meetings. Where possible, assessments should be based on predefined rules and scored on some reasonably objective basis.

Once the short list, of perhaps five practices, has been agreed, then the communication process needs to become more formal. At this stage only hard facts and details of information passed to the bidder should be shared. Personal impressions should be retained by the individual team member to support their evaluation of the bids. At this stage contact with bidders ought to be restricted to answering their questions with regard to the tender, so as to avoid accusations of collusion or preferential treatment. All discussions with the bidder should be recorded at the time and placed in the bidder's file.

Once bids have been received there should be no discussion with the bidders until the presentation, except to clarify the format of the presentation and to resolve any questions the selection committee may have from the proposals. These latter discussions will again be filed. There should be no further discussions with bidders until after the final choice is made.

After the final selection there will almost certainly be the need to negotiate the terms of reference and the contract with the favoured adviser. At this stage a principal negotiator should be appointed and, as far as possible, all discussions with the consultant should be made with that person present. Any other discussions should be recorded and passed to the chief negotiator. All discussions must be recorded and all agreements and decisions formalised in writing between client and adviser.

Agree the rules

Once the committee is formed it must agree the rules both for its own purposes and for the bid process that it will adopt for the selection. It will have to decide on the criteria for the following:

- selecting the long list;

- reducing that to a short list of invited bidders;

- the evaluation criteria for the bids, which will be derived from the project definition and invitation documents;

- the presentation evaluation rules, which will be defined after the bids have been evaluated but before the presentations.

Consultancy approach required

The committee need to decide what style of consultancy they are seeking. There are essentially three main types:

- **The expert.** The adviser comes in, undertakes their analysis and then tells the client what to do. Frequently the problem is that the client does not properly understand the recommendation and the implementation is therefore not entirely successful.

- **The tight brief.** The client gives a very tight brief to the consultant with a clearly defined result. These tend to have a high failure rate because they do not make full use of the consultant's skills and do not address the underlying real needs of the client. As a rule these projects tend to be undertaken for the wrong reasons, often simply to promote an individual or departmental view or to meet some other internal political agenda.

■ **The partnership.** This has gained much favour in recent years and is proving successful where there is a genuine commitment on both sides to achieve the best result. It may start with a single project where consultant and client staff work side by side to some extent appropriate to the project. If the relationship works and the adviser has a suitable spread of skills available, a longer term strategic partnership may be formed. The client gets continuity and does not have to explain everything for each project to a new set of advisers; the consultant gets a steady flow of business and the opportunity to see their ideas properly implemented. Both avoid the substantial time spent on the selection process. The relationship has to be managed carefully to avoid the feeling that the client is being milked or that they are dependent on the consultant. Of course there is always the opportunity to switch to competitive tendering if such problems arise.

115

Selection criteria

At an early meeting the selection team should decide on some of the broad selection criteria. Clearly these will include the technical skills required for the work, but they should also include the cultural compatibility of client and consultant. Whilst the detailed evaluation criteria will be developed as the specification is developed, some judgements have to be made with regard to both the initial list of possible firms and, more especially, the short list to be invited to bid.

Identifying possible advisers

■ ■ ■

The first challenge facing someone planning to use consultants, especially if it is for the first time, is to actually find the names and details of suitable candidates. Having identified a need for special external advice there are many sources, both formal and informal, that can be used.

Creating the initial long list

Using contacts

Many client managers have a wide network of contacts in similar organisations to their own. Some of these will have faced or be facing similar problems and may well have already used consultants themselves. So as a starting point the would-be user of professional advisers can let this network know they are looking for a firm with a particular set of skills. This route has the advantages of both enabling the prospective buyer to have suitable advisers recommended, and also providing them with informal advice as to who to avoid. Over and above the list of consultants there will be considerable free advice on everything from the selection process to the management and implementation of the project. Some of this will be good, some of it will have to be treated with caution. Like a consultant, one of a manager's key skills is their judgement and ability to assess the value of offered information. That said, your own professional network is a useful source of advice and certainly should be used.

Consultant's tip

Whether it is a new accountant, or someone who can provide advice on a highly esoteric aspect of your business, all organisations need to find new professional advisers from time to time. So you can usefully start collecting information now, even if you do not have an immediate need. Start by maintaining an index of specialists who might be relevant to your work in some way. The list can be built up from people who write to you, recommendations from colleagues and associates, references in journals or at institute meetings. It does not have to be highly organised, as long as you can get at the right people when the need arises. Keep the list simple or you will not maintain it.

I would suggest keeping cuttings, business cards and notes on scraps of paper in two or three wallet files, probably one for each broad grouping, say: general business advisers, technical advisers and anybody else. Whenever you see an adviser mentioned in a paper who may be useful in the future, cut the article out and drop it in the wallet. When you need an adviser pull out the appropriate wallet, browse its contents and start your initial long list with anybody who might be appropriate to the current requirement. At this stage do not worry about being too accurate – you will add to the list further before reducing it to a more manageable list of suitable candidates.

117

Libraries

Most reasonable-sized towns and cities have a business library with many of the main directories listing specialists in all sorts of fields, from publishing to high technology. Some of these will list consultancy firms and their specialism, others will supply a lead to organisations that may be able to provide a list of suitable advisers.

Organisations that may help

Such organisations are of two kinds: first there are the organisations that support the professions, amongst whose members there may be those that offer their services as advisers or consultants. Not all their members will be able to provide such advice, as many will be employed to provide in-house expertise. However, the case study below illustrates how the The Ergonomics Society handles such varied interests. Their approach is fairly typical, although some professional bodies, such as the Institute of Chartered Accounts and Institute of Management Consultants go rather further and publish guidance for any potential client seeking to commission the sort of professional advice that their members can give.

Consultant's Casebook

THE ERGONOMICS SOCIETY

The Ergonomics Society is fairly typical of a small specialist professional body and learned society. It has just over a thousand members and is run by a small part-time staff and volunteers. It holds a database of members and the areas in which they specialise and information on whether they are able and prepared to work on a consultancy basis.

The Society accepts enquiries from prospective clients, but because of their small staff, they prefer these to be in writing. They do have some general literature about the Society and its aims, and guidance on what ergonomists do. Because of their small number of members, they can usually guide a potential client to someone suitable who can undertake the necessary work on a consultancy basis. However because there is a growing need, the Society is formalising its consultancy register. This may have been launched by the time this book is published. They are adopting a strict accreditation process and setting quality standards for those members who wish to practise as consultants. The basic professional register requires two referees from prospective members, who must have followed a recognised qualifying course. The register of practitioners also requires more experience, and those members included on the consultancy register will consist of fully qualified practitioners who have been further vetted by three senior members of the Society.

> Many professional associations adopt a similar approach,
> although The Ergonomics Society are, perhaps, adopting a
> stricter accreditation regime than many.

Trade associations and professional bodies

Many of the trade associations and professional bodies repre-
senting the client's industry or profession will provide advice,
and may maintain lists of suppliers of all sorts of services.
These lists may not only be of consultants and advisers, but
many include those offering everything from computer software to equipment. The advisers on such lists will usually
have strong industry knowledge. This can be of considerable
benefit but you should be aware of the pitfalls: if the consultant's experience is entirely in the industry they may lack the
breadth of vision that the client is seeking to address. Indeed,
with the trend towards flatter management structures many
consultants who specialise in particular industries may have
spent all their working life as middle or senior managers in
that industry. They may have only gone into consultancy as a
result of redundancy, rather than a desire to be a consultant.
Whilst many of these people will make excellent consultants,
a would-be client would be well advised to check very carefully that such industry experts possess true consultancy
expertise and understanding of the wider business aspects of
their knowledge. In some cases a client should actively seek
an outsider to provide fresh thinking and, hopefully, innovative solutions that give real competitive advantage.

Referrals

Probably the most valuable source for anyone choosing consultants is referrals from colleagues both within one's own
organisation and from similar organisations. Established
consultancy firms work hard to build a reputation which
encourages such referrals. Most successful practices get a
significant part of their business from referrals by satisfied

119

clients. So referrals are good for the would-be user of consultancy and for the consultants themselves.

Advertising

It is sometimes appropriate to advertise seeking expressions of interest from consultancy firms who feel competent to undertake the proposed project. This is a common approach in public-sector procurement. The over-riding reason is openness and equality of opportunity for all potential bidders. Within the European Union open procurement processes are enshrined in EU/GATT regulations for public procurement. These regulations set limits above which projects must be advertised in the *European Journal* and be handled in an open and auditable manner. Whilst it does add extra work to the procurement process its considerable benefit lies in providing an auditable process that minimises the opportunity for discrimination. Indeed, if the regulations are not followed an unsuccessful bidder can seek to have the contract that has been awarded overturned by the Courts.

Whilst there are several different forms of recognised procurement procedure under the regulations, it is common for expressions of interest to be sought from suitably qualified organisations. The expressions of interest usually seek to establish the basic financial standing, qualification and experience of the potential bidder. They confirm that the bidder has what is needed to undertake the work and that they comply with appropriate standards (from quality procedures to equal opportunities in employment). By seeking expressions of interest one avoids having to distribute to all and sundry large numbers of substantial documents containing commercially sensitive, if not actually confidential, information. Instead a detailed document inviting bids and setting out the scope and nature of the work to be undertaken need only be sent to those bodies that have been prequalified. This also avoids the need for many firms to spend a lot of time and money preparing proposals that have little chance of success. Even so, that cost must still be borne in mind when selecting a short list of bid-

120

ders from their expressions of interest. Without doubt the number invited should be less than ten, and five or six is probably a more appropriate upper limit. If it is not possible to limit invited bidders to that sort of number, then the request for expressions of interest and the subsequent evaluation was not sufficiently well thought through. When inviting bids you should feel that any of those invited would be capable of the work from the point of view of resources and quality. You are then simply seeking to confirm their approach, costs and the personal relationship that can be established with their team who will be doing the work.

Consultant's tip

In selecting a short list of potential advisers there is one particular source I would recommend you treat with considerable care. That is the friend of a friend. Especially the friend of a friend who has a son or daughter doing a course in ... I have undertaken more than enough troubleshooting projects, especially in relation to computer systems, as a result of advice from such sources. Often it is a case of a little knowledge being dangerous. The person providing the advice did not have the experience or breadth of knowledge needed to undertake the work or to appreciate the difficulties they might encounter, both technical and, more especially, the people issues.

Whilst from my point of view such work is at a premium rate, it is pretty soul-destroying and I would sooner not have to do it. One has an unhappy client, possibly with managers whose jobs are at risk as a consequence. There is also a youngster whose career has possibly been blighted. All because the client tried to cut corners. Be warned.

121

Brokerage services

There are brokerage services of various types. Many professional associations have some form of service to clients looking for consultants in their discipline. These vary in formality. They may have a list of members who are prepared and able to act as consultants – not all of whom will be available as some will be employed as in-house experts. Alternatively, they may have a full service with full-time staff to help the client choose the most appropriate consultant.

Other services

There are others services, usually sponsored by government departments or government agencies, such as Business Links, Training and Enterprise Councils (TECs) and Local Enterprise Companies. Coupled with those, Chambers of Commerce and local government development agencies may be able to suggest advisers who are based or operating in their areas.

Telephone directories

Finally, of course, there are the Yellow Pages and the Business Pages, but these give little guidance beyond a name and telephone number. If you need a local service, these may be an initial starting point, but you will need to telephone for more information.

Narrow down to a short list

Having developed an initial list, you will quickly want to trim it down to manageable proportions, possibly in stages. You will be able to rule out some very easily from initial contacts by telephone and face to face, or they will rule themselves out. For example they may not have the skills and resources necessary, or they may not be available at the right time.

Consultant's tip

Use any initial contact, even by telephone, to judge the organisation. Score them on some simple basis, say 0 = not offered, 1 = partly satisfactory, 2 = entirely satisfactory. I would typically score them for aspects such as:

- friendly and professional manner;
- know their services and products;

- *answer or return calls quickly;*

- *answer my questions fully and admit gaps in their knowledge;*

- *willingness to respond or meet;*

- *do not leap to conclusions;*

- *do not force their agenda;*

- *they listen;*

- *I think I like them!*

At this stage any judgement will be very superficial and subjective. But we have to start the selection process somewhere. I have carried out a lot of procurement of services on behalf of clients and I cannot think of a case using this approach where we dropped someone we should not have done.

If I have made it clear that I am looking to buy a service and a supplier does not come back to me, I do not pursue them. If they cannot follow up on a call from a new customer, why should I believe that they will follow through on anything?

123

Another aspect of selection is to choose horses for courses. If you are a small owner-run business operating in a local market it is probably undesirable to use a large international firm of advisers which advises multinationals and government, even if they would take you on. They would be too expensive and would probably not have sufficient experience of businesses like yours. Instead you should use someone who works in your field much of the time and who is used to the very particular problems of small and medium-sized enterprises.

The converse is also true – if you are looking for someone with international experience do not use a firm that has no experience outside their home town. Note that this is not an issue of the size of the firm; some of the world's leading experts work in small partnerships or even on their own from their home. Choose someone who is able to demonstrate achievement in similar circumstances to your own.

Consultant's tip

At all costs avoid arrogant consultants who claim to know it all, especially in relation to your business and your industry. Choose instead people with whom you can quickly develop some empathy. A good consultant will put themselves into your shoes without jumping to conclusions or losing their objectivity. They will be able to tell you the hard things but do so whilst respecting your business and personal philosophies.

Ask yourself whether you like this person, and could have a joke with them when you have more problems than solutions. If the answer is yes and they have the necessary background, you may well have found your adviser (or at least one of them).

Detailing the project or problem
■ ■ ■

A key task is defining the problem or the project that you need undertaken. You have to make it clear and put boundaries on it whilst giving the bidders room to be innovative in the way they propose to deliver the service. Also, you need to give room for creative solutions yet still not give an unscrupulous adviser room to do whatever they fancy rather than what you need.

How do you do this? There is no one simple answer that applies across all disciplines. All I can do is give you a few guiding principles to allow you to develop your own approach to your own problem. And I am afraid that you may need a completely new approach for the next one.

I have therefore come up with a new acronym for the purpose: SCOPE. It is made up as follows:

- **Symptoms not solutions.** Detail the symptoms and the supporting facts but do not suggest possible solutions. Solutions are what you are asking the adviser to determine from their analysis, experience and their understanding of your capability.

- **Clarity.** Do not try to get clever with the problem definition. Describe it simply and in your own terms. If it is industry specific you may wish to avoid jargon to allow experts from outside your own industry to understand, so that you can get some cross-fertilisation from other sectors.

- **Options.** Keep your options open as far as the solution is concerned. Look at the extracts from the Consultant's Casebook; many of them rely for success on a consultant being able to move across different disciplines, for example, from computing to work practices, from sales to computing and so on.

- **Precise.** Detail the specific points you need to be covered but do not make your specification so tight that you effectively prejudge the answers. You need to put constraints on the study to be undertaken but make sure that these constraints are not artificial.

- **Essential facts** – include them all. Make the definition as complete as possible without sacrificing the points above. Within reason, the more relevant knowledge the prospective consultant is given the better. It is easier (and safer) to ignore something irrelevant than to make assumptions from incomplete information.

By sticking to these principles you will not go far wrong. The adviser should have enough information to ask the right questions and from that make a good judgement as to what they need to propose.

Inviting proposals

■ ■ ■

The invitation document

The following paragraphs describe the content of the invitation document.

Summary

All documents should include a one-page summary setting out the key points. An invitation to tender is no exception. As a consultant I want to be able to assess quickly whether I will want to bid for the work – the summary will help me to do so. Usually I speak to the client beforehand; I establish that the work falls within my firm's competence and that we expect to have the necessary resources available at the time the client requires them. However, sometimes when responding to advertisements I have to rely on the documents and the summary is especially helpful. Also, from time to time we receive invitations out of the blue. Usually these invitations are from organisations where we have pre-qualified for possible work – when something more or less suitable arises they send us the documents and we have to decide whether to bid for it or not. The summary helps us to establish whether we even need to read the document or talk to the client.

126

Background to the organisation

I like to have a reasonable amount of background history of the organisation and where it sees its future, especially if it is a new client. Also I like to get a feel for the organisation's values and culture. As I do quite a lot of work in the not-for-profit sector this aspect is particularly important, but its importance should not be under-estimated even for commercial organisations.

The background to the organisation will then lead on to the project brief.

Project brief

This is the meat in the sandwich; it determines the nature and scope of the work. Much of the rest of the invitation document will be standard, but the project brief has to be written for each commission.

It is essential that great care and thought is given to this section. This will determine the scope and cost of the proposals.

You do not want to waste your time on proposals that do not meet your needs or which you cannot afford. You have to give the advisers the chance really to understand what you want out of the project, when you would like it and what sort of budget you are working within. However, first and foremost the project brief should be the client's view of the project.

Whilst you need to put boundaries on the work, you also need to balance this with the need to allow room for the consultants to be innovative. We have already discussed the importance of innovation in a fast changing world. If you set out in detail how the consultant is to approach the work you might as well have done it in-house. If you are too prescriptive you will not be using all the talents of your advisers and you may even discourage the best from bidding because they may believe the quality of their work will be compromised.

127

Background to the project
The background should set out why the organisation has decided that this work needs doing, or the broad nature of the problem. It should give any history that might be relevant and it should be honest and open. If poor decisions were made, or worse, they should be mentioned – the consultant is going to find out, so be open about it.

Objectives
The organisation needs to be clear about what it expects from the proposed project. The objectives might be a set of strategic objectives, a clear statement of the purpose of the organisation or even a project definition and scope to resolve a problem. But the client must have a clear idea of what they want to achieve from the work. How else will the client and the consultant know whether the work has been completed, let alone whether it was successful or not?

Sometimes, although the work is being commissioned by the client it may be for purposes outside the client organisation. If that is the case then the uses to which reports and other documents may be put need to be stated with great clarity.

Most advisers' contracts limit the use of reports to internal use only and require the client to seek written permission before using them for other purposes. If you know that reports will be required for use outside the organisation then you should make this clear in the invitation to tender.

The reasons for this limitation are to do, mainly, with professional indemnity and insurance. If the report is made available to a third party and used to support a decision – a merger or take-over, say – which then goes wrong, then the consultant could face litigation. Also, the style and emphasis of a document for third-party purposes may well differ from that appropriate for limited circulation within the organisation. This difference in style is not to cover anything up, but simply because different audiences require different styles to convey the same message.

Project timetable

If there is a deadline for completion of the work then it should be stated. It may be that there is simply a desire to have the work completed by a specific date, if possible, or it may be needed for the AGM or to meet a deadline imposed by the needs of a customer of the client. The consultants may suggest in their bids that the given date is not possible, in which case the client has learned something and either has to limit the scope of the work or accept later completion.

A broad timetable is useful, as it allows the consultant to get a feel for the scope of the project and, maybe, to balance their own resources with other commitments. Both will have an effect on the final price.

Tender rules

The invitation should clearly set out the rules that need to be followed by bidders. Some will be about who can do what with the report and the findings of the project.

Sealed bids

It is not uncommon for bids to be required in sealed form. These are opened at a formal, sometimes public, meeting of the selection committee. This is most common for public-sector procurement, where strict equal opportunity rules apply and the compliance with the procedures must be auditable.

If the bid is to be made in this way it is usual to require submission in supplied packaging, with no external marks that might identify the bidder. Usually if the bidder breaks any of these rules then the bid will not be considered.

Format of the document

I would strongly recommend that you specify the required format of the proposals. This will make it easier to compare the bids with each other and to score them against pre-defined evaluation criteria.

How far you take this specification is up to you – I have seen invitations to tender which required compliance with each detailed element to be marked by the bidder as 'fully', 'in part' or 'not at all'. Tedious for me as a consultant, but I am sure that it made scoring the bids very easy. However, this approach does not allow the bidder to innovate and come up with a better approach than has been envisaged by the client. The easy scoring benefits probably mean extra work at specification stage and almost certainly produce a less than ideal solution in the end.

I would suggest that you detail the required structure of the document down to chapter and section level, with some detailed requirement with regard to the way the timetable and fees are presented (see Appendix D). However, I would also recommend that you allow additional information to be included as an annex to the main document. This will allow the bidder to personalise the bid and give you an insight into their style and culture.

Finally, ask for a one-page summary, which must include an overview of the project timetable and the total fees including expenses. One proposal I was asked to provide required a one-page tender document, for a project worth nearly £100,000!

The client asked for other background information to be appended to the one-page bid. It can be done.

Information required

The information that you require to assess the bid should be detailed. This should include the following:

- total fees, including all expenses;
- CVs for all main team members;
- timetable and phasing;
- resources required from client;
- financial details of the organisation;
- management structure;
- accreditations, references;
- approach to the work and methodologies;
- expected outcomes (measurable wherever possible);
- deliverables;
- project management approach.

Selection process

Make the selection process clear and explain the steps you are taking.

Timetable for bids

Make the timetable clear and do not forget to include dates for:

- bidders' workshop;
- closing date for bids;
- decision day for final short list;
- presentation dates;
- final decision;
- project start.

Equal opportunities

If you have policies that require suppliers to have their own equal opportunity policies for staff recruitment, then be specific.

You may wish to demand certification of no collusive bidding. This is where two or more firms agree not to compete in specific sectors, on particular projects or on some form of rota basis. They may or may not share the work that each wins under such arrangements. This arrangement may be just to make it easier for all members of the cartel by their not having to spend a lot of time on expensive proposals: they share the work by each bidding in turn. However, collusive bidding is illegal in most countries and is certainly so under European Union law against cartels. If allowed to take place it makes a mockery of the open tendering process. Public-sector procurement often requires a certificate to say that collusive bidding has not taken place.

131

Bribes

The other form of collusion that you will wish to avoid is between your own staff and a bidder usually involving bribes. Again I have often been asked for certification of this on public-sector procurement. Many organisations, both public and private sector, have very strict rules about gifts to staff from suppliers. If I buy a pub lunch for anyone from my public-sector clients they will insist on reciprocating the next time.

Work-place rules

If you have strict work-place rules for employees, then you should make it clear in the invitation to bid that all consultants will be expected to comply with them at all times.

Many organisations are non-smoking, and if that is the case then this rule should be explained to prospective consultants. If smoking is allowed, say when and where it is permissible.

Alcohol and drugs are also an issue in an increasing number of organisations. For example, for some time British Rail has applied the same rules about drugs and alcohol to all its staff. For many years this only applied to train crew, but as part of an equalisation of terms and conditions it was made all-encompassing. Anyone with more than the permitted amount of alcohol in their blood can be dismissed. As a result, there is no lunch-time drinking and staff are careful if they have been at a party until late the night before. Consultants are expected to follow the same rules.

If personal identity is a requirement for staff then you may wish to make it a requirement for advisers. Will you provide identity badges or do you expect the consultancy firm to provide their own? Spell this out at this stage.

Your aim should be to avoid surprises when the consultant starts that might cause them difficulty. The earlier they are told of an issue, the less room there is for them to complain. If all the information is complete at the bid stage, then the consultant will have a lot more confidence that they will not walk into any nasty surprises – you can help to allay the consultant's fears.

Intellectual property

One should consider intellectual property rights for many consultancy roles. These not only include copyright and patents, but also designs and other ideas that may not be formally protected.

Each specialism will tend to have its own approach to these rights. Generally consultants will seek to keep them for themselves. As far as copyright is concerned, that will usually be correct, as transfer of copyright can only be made by the originator; it cannot be taken by default. There are certain exceptions about work for hire which might apply to contract staff. The work for hire rules are intended to give employers copyright of any work performed by their staff as part of their employment. As we have already said, a true consultant is not in any way to be mistaken for a member of the client's staff, contract or otherwise; therefore they should retain copyright in their work.

If necessary, the work can be licensed to the client or transferred to them, although for most business advisers this is not an issue. There is implicit licensing in the terms under which the reports may be used by the client. However, those consultants, designers, etc. who work in the more creative areas will usually have standard contract terms with regard to copyright. Indeed, there may be established practices within their industries, although that is not to say that the rules cannot be changed, usually at a price!

Patents and rights to patent inventions will be an issue for people like designers and engineers who are asked to produce design work for clients. In such cases there needs to be negotiation before the event on how any patentable inventions are to be handled. Again, there will be custom and practice within the industry. However, it is essential that if there is any possibility of such patentable invention then the terms should be agreed in advance.

133

There is also an issue that should be addressed with regard to innovation, ideas and concepts outside the scope of copyright or patent law. Both client and consultant should seek to maintain good relationships throughout the project and afterwards, so I would recommend that agreement is reached on who can use any such material and any limitations on how it should be used. Some of the material used by the consultant may be of considerable commercial value, so they might not wish it to be made publicly available. In such cases it may be appropriate to allow the other party to use it for internal use, but not externally for commercial or other purposes.

Goodwill on both sides will find a mutually acceptable solution. For much business advice these matters are not an issue at all.

Official Secrets Act and confidentiality
You should make clear the confidentiality rules and, of course, if the Official Secrets Act applies. If the Act does apply you may also need to point out that any bidding organisation and its staff agree to accept any security vetting procedures that may be required.

Limitations on use of the report

If, as already mentioned, a report is to be used outside the organisation this should be made clear. This is because the client will have to consider issues with respect to their indemnity insurance and litigation. For example, if the report is used to support a merger bid which subsequently goes wrong, then the consultant could face a considerable claim for compensation. The costs could be out of all proportion to the fee, or indeed to the consultant's insurance cover.

Insu3nce cover

You may need to set out what protection you require from the bidder. This will normally include third-party risks and cover damage caused to the client's property, staff and visitors by the consultancy firm's staff and sub-contractors. A level may need to be specified appropriate to the nature of your business and property.

Professional indemnity

You may also wish to specify a level of cover for the consequence of poor or negligent advice. This should not be a standard blanket figure, but should match the risk to the client, taking into account the business of the client, the scale and nature of the advice being sought and the clarity of the terms of reference. Bear in mind that, as a manager, you will be taking the decisions and the consultant should only be providing advice on the basis of the terms of reference and information provided by client's staff.

Prepare evaluation criteria and approach

By the closing date for the receipt of bids you should have prepared and documented the evaluation criteria and the method to be used to assess the proposals.

These may vary from a brief list of key points to a highly structured formal scoring method. Again, the more objective the assessment procedure can be made the less scope there will be for dispute, and it will also be more auditable. This is particularly important for organisations in the public sector who have to be able to demonstrate proper use of public monies. It is also an issue for many others with strict policies on equality of opportunity.

Clearly, in deciding on an approach, judgement has to come into play – one would not use the same method for a simple two-day project as one would for a major strategic redefinition of the business involving a team of advisers for a year or more.

Included as Appendix F is a method I use when selecting suppliers on behalf of clients. It has the virtue that it can be scaled from a simple single level for a small project to many levels with complex weighting for major procurement.

Initial contact

Remember that a good consultant will listen more than talk in the early stages. They will also ask questions rather than make statements. They will be seeking to understand the issues, your business and your objectives for the work. The consultant will not come out with glib solutions or say, 'the problem is just like one I had at ...'.

A good consultant will not need to push a solution from the start. If the consultant you are meeting starts to do so, avoid them as they will almost certainly push their standard solutions whether they are right for you or not.

Consultant's tip

Start your evaluation with your first contact with the consultancy firm. Initial contact will probably be by telephone, so the aspects you need to consider are as follows:

- *Was the telephone answered promptly and was the receptionist pleasant and helpful? Were you put through to the right person first time and without fuss? If the person*

▶

▶

> *you needed was not in was whoever you spoke to helpful and did the right person ring back as promised?*
>
> ■ *When you got through to the main contact were they interested in your project and your organisation? Or were they cool and indifferent? Did they give you time on the telephone or were you rushed? Did they ask for the bid documents or, even better, ask to meet you to discuss your needs?*
>
> ■ *If you discussed the broad needs on the telephone did the consultant seek to try and suggest they knew the answers; were they jumping to glib solutions?*
>
> *The initial contact will often show the real character of an organisation before they get into polished sales mode!*

136

Query handling

Advisers who are going to bid will need all the information that they can get, and almost certainly more than is in the invitation documents. They will need to be able to clarify points and check their understanding of the requirements. This process may need to involve senior members of your selection team.

The simplest way to meet this need is to provide a contact name and telephone number. This does not have to be a senior person, but it should be someone who is readily available – especially as the deadline for submission approaches and the bidders need to clarify last-minute points. The principal contact for queries should have a good understanding of the project requirements, and if they are the person who prepared the bid invitation, all the better.

At this stage good documentation procedures become important. It is essential that you do not inadvertently give advantage to one bidder by giving more or different information in response to a similar question. If they do not ask the right questions, that can be unfortunate for them; but if two bid-

ders ask the same question they should get the same information. This can be ensured if you have notes, either of the
discussion with the previous questioner or a list of prepared
responses to anticipated questions. (If you can anticipate
questions, you might consider whether the answers should
have been in the documents.)

If a major issue arises, either as a result of a question, or from
external circumstances, you may wish to send all invited bidders additional invitation by post or facsimile. It is in your
interests as the client for the bids to be as complete and accurate as possible – that means that they must be based on the
best information available.

If the project is large or complex, then it may be appropriate
to set up a bidders' conference to explain the requirements
and to answer questions. In this way all bidders who are
interested enough to attend will get the same information;
the process can then be seen to be fair and above suspicion of
bias. This can also be a way of ensuring all bidders have
access to the in-house technical specialists who might otherwise be difficult to reach.

In any case, a prospective bidder, especially if the firm does
not already work for the client, may wish to meet to discuss
the details. There may be several reasons in the consultant's
mind for doing so. I have already discussed the importance of
personal relationships and mutual regard in successful consultancy projects – the meeting could help to establish such
regard. The consultant may want to find out about the background to the decision-making process by identifying the
decision makers, their personal drivers and any other political aspects to the decision. Consultants may also simply want
to know what competition they are up against; as a general
rule I would suggest that you be open about the number
asked to bid but not about their identities, so that the bidder
cannot pitch their fees on the basis of the competition. (This
can also be a good reason for having a known low-cost firm in
the short list!)

Consultant's tip

Sometimes you may be asked how many are bidding, or may be asked to make a presentation when you only have one suitable bidder. In such cases you need to retain a competitive pressure on the bidder, but not to tell any lies.

In such circumstances I suggest that you simply tell the bidder that there will be no more than three, five or whatever in the short list. This is true, and it leaves the consultants having to make a competitive pitch for the work.

More usually, the consultant is simply trying to get a feel for the client's expectations with regard to scope and timescale for the project. They may ask about the client's budget but again you should be circumspect about revealing any details. It may be appropriate (the selection committee will have to decide), to give a very general expected fee range, but do not reveal the actual expected or maximum budget. You want the fees to be based on the work involved, you do not want the work and fees based on the budget you have. You want to put the bidder under some pressure to be creative about how they will solve your problem.

Anyone in your organisation who is likely to speak to the bidders needs to know what the rules are for divulging information and who can say what.

Although the bidder may be seeking to gain some advantage from meetings with the client, you should treat these as part of the evaluation process. If the bidder is too aggressive in seeking information and does not appear prepared to respect your wish to keep some information confidential, then you may have to score them down on their attitude to you as a client.

Sending out tender documents

The invitation to bid should allow a reasonable time for submission of proposals. For small straightforward projects two weeks is probably sufficient; any less is too tight for the bidders to give the project proper consideration. For very large bids you probably have enough experience and support not to need my assistance. For the rest I would consider three weeks sufficient and a month too long. You are, after all, trying to see how the bidding firms respond under pressure; can they deliver when the heat is on?

The covering letter need only be brief and I would recommend that it reiterates the deadline for submission of bids, the address to which they should be sent, whether there are any rules about using supplied packaging for the proposal and who to contact for further information.

Consultant's tip

In your contacts with possible advisory firms, were they making it easy for you to buy from them or were they putting up obstacles?

We are often told how difficult new business is to come by, yet I am amazed how difficult some companies make it to buy their products and services. This is true of all types of business, including consultancies, and on your evaluation you should score down any firm that does not positively seek to make it easy for you as a client.

Presentations
■ ■ ■

Beauty parades – arguments for and against them

Bear in mind that presentations will take out several of your senior managers for a substantial amount of time: probably a minimum of three days, and possibly more. Do you really need a formal presentation, or would something simpler be more appropriate?

Preparation

If a presentation is going to work well, then it needs careful planning and management by the client. You have to ensure that the facilities that are promised to the bidders are available. These typically include an overhead projector, perhaps a 35mm slide projector, a flip chart easel, paper and pens.

You will already have determined the format, say thirty minutes of presentation by the bidder and then an hour of discussion. You will have advised the short-listed firms of this. Before the day, you need to make decisions about who will chair the sessions - for consistency, it should be the same person all the way through.

Try to arrange the timing of presentations so that there is a quarter to half an hour interval between them. This will give you time to share any initial thoughts, clear the room (do not forget to remove any flip charts that were drawn), and avoid having the bidding firms trip over each other.

You also have to decide on your questions and who will ask them. There are two schools of thought with regard to questions: the first says that the same questions should be asked of all presenting firms; the second says that you should ask questions that will clarify each individual proposal. I believe the latter is more useful, as the first may cause you to ask questions that have been answered in some of the proposals. Adopting the second approach does not preclude the use of the same question in all presentations – there will be points for which you require a definitive statement and so will require the same questions asked in exactly the same way.

Finally, you need to agree on the style of the sessions. Are they going to be stiff and formal, with deadpan faces all round and a lot of pressure on the bidder? Or will they be more relaxed and affable with the intention of encouraging the bidder to open up because their guard is down? It does not really matter which style you choose, and will probably make no difference to what you will learn if you have experienced, professional advisers in front of you. My recommendation

would be to be yourselves. You are looking for a consultant
who can fit in with the culture and style of your organisation;
it will be much easier to assess that if you are behaving normally. You can then see how the presentation team responds
to your style. If they are quickly at ease and start to adopt a
similar demeanour, then you will be well on the way to finding the right consultant for you.

Evaluation criteria

You also need to define the evaluation criteria, and I would
suggest that you incorporate them into the same model as
that used for the proposals. At the proposal stage the
presentation will be unscored and the same for all bidders.
After the presentation the model will be updated and a
revised score calculated – it is now a case of winner takes
all.

141

On the day

Ensure that somebody is at the presentation venue in good
time to ensure that the room is properly set up, all the facilities work, and there are pens for the flip chart, etc. (I always
take my own when I am making one of these presentations –
just in case). Are tea and coffee to be available?

You should also brief the receptionists so that they know what
to expect, understand the waiting arrangements, and know
how to get the bidding teams to and from the presentation
room without them meeting (if you wish to retain confidentiality).

Check that the heating is comfortable and that the seats are
arranged in a way that is reasonably friendly but not so com-
pact that those presenting can read what the client team are
writing!

> *Consultant's tip*
>
> *All the consultants I know are expert at reading upside down. I myself have often found out who I am up against by reading the list of those attending on the receptionist's pad. It is an ability that comes in useful in all sorts of circumstances!*

What you see is what you get

Check that the presentation team are listed in the proposal as the people who will actually do the work. If any of them is not, then ask 'why not?' and seek confirmation that they will be undertaking a significant part of your work.

Similarly, if there are any key people missing, then again you need to know why. Work hard on both these situations; you are going to be working with these people for some time, so knowing that they will be able to fit in with you and your staff is essential. If the person missing is a highly technical specialist, it may be because they are not very commercial and do not perform well in business situations. In this case it is important that you meet them before awarding the contract, so that you can make a judgement about their ability to work in the team.

Negotiation
■ ■ ■

Public-sector procurement

Public-sector procurement is broadly similar to the process described here. This process is used largely unchanged, for contracts with values of less than certain limits specified in the regulations. The limits are revised regularly and vary for different kinds of supply. Where the value is such that full open purchasing rules apply, then the process is different, as described below.

With few exceptions, the first step is to post a notice in the *Journal of the European Union* announcing the contract to be awarded. Suppliers are requested to make a formal expression of interest, with some limited details of their financial standing and expertise with relation to the contract. Alternatively, they may be asked to send for the documents describing the project and to bid in the same way as we have described earlier.

On receipt of the expressions of interest, a selection is made on a basis agreed in advance – usually with regard to financial standing and, perhaps, basic competence to undertake the work. From then on the process is as described earlier, using the firms short-listed from the expression of interest as the short list of firms invited to bid.

The aim is then to determine which suppliers are fully able to undertake the work. Fees are considered, but would not, at this stage, be the final arbiter. After the presentation, all those firms who appear able to perform the work satisfactorily negotiate a memorandum of specification and contract terms. In the case of advisers, these are effectively the terms of reference and the associated contract, respectively.

143

At this stage, the final short list of suppliers (usually no more than three, sometimes only one) are sent an invitation to tender against the memorandum of specification. This final stage has a short deadline and requires limited documentation, as all the terms except the fee to be paid are included in the memorandum which forms part of the contract.

Once the final tenders are in, the contract is awarded to the bidder with the lowest price. Remember that all suppliers at this stage are deemed to be fully capable of producing what is required, so price is the only determinant left.

You may think that you can avoid the need for the open purchasing procedure by breaking the work into several smaller projects below the threshold. However, there are rules under which related projects or purchases can be aggregated to determine whether the threshold is reached. If contracts are awarded that could have fallen under this regime, these contracts can be tested in the courts – an expensive and time-consuming exercise. So the rules need to be respected and understood.

Executive summary

Traditionally, professional advisers have been selected on the basis of recommendation by friend or colleagues. With the growing importance of the ability to demonstrate sound corporate governance, clients are increasingly turning to competitive tendering, sometimes known as 'beauty parades'. Such an approach has both benefits and disadvantages. In most cases there is more to be gained than to be lost through competition.

The selection process is not complex, although there are many potential pitfalls. To gain the full benefits you need to adopt a structured process and to follow it logically and completely. If you take any short cuts then many of the benefits such as the ability to audit the choice of adviser and the selection process may disappear.

A selection committee needs to be appointed to oversee the process and to evaluate the proposals and presentations from prospective advisers. They need to set the timetable, rules, evaluation criteria and to prepare the invitation documents. For it to be effective, the members of the selection team must give the process a substantial amount of time.

The invitation document must be as complete as possible. In particular, it must set out clearly the scope and nature of the work, and most importantly, describe the objectives in a manner that can be measured. It is essential that the document is robust, as it will form part of the final contract and will be the basis for monitoring the performance of the consultant.

The criteria by which the proposals will be assessed will be developed from the invitation to tender. This needs to be done before bids are received if strict auditability is to be maintained. Similarly, a set of evaluation criteria are needed for presentations by the final short list of potential advisers.

The procurement process as described is similar to that adopted for any major procurement. It is equally applicable to the private and public sector, as well as for not-for-profit bodies such as charities and housing associations. There are some possible difference for public-sector organisations where the European Union regulations for public procurement come into play.

Checklist

1 Collect information on possible advisers and consultants who are doing work in your industry in areas of relevance to your organisation. Do this just in case you need new advisers.

2 Identify any issue that cannot be handled in house. Then describe them sufficiently to determine what skills will be needed to resolve them.

3 Appoint a selection committee to manage the selection process and, possibly, the subsequent implementation of recommendations.

4 Draw up a long list of potential suppliers. Have the selection committee agree the rules for reducing this to a short list. The short list of those invited to bid should be of no more than five.

5 Define the problem in more detail – apply SCOPE to the definition.

6 The selection team should agree the timetable, the evaluation approach and criteria, and how bidder's queries are to be handled.

7 Prepare for the presentation whilst waiting for the bids. Resolve queries as agreed previously.

8 Receive proposals and evaluate against agreed criteria. Notify the final short list of firms to make presentations of no more than two or three of the date, time and place, and agree what facilities they will require for their presentation.

9 Complete preparation of questions and evaluation criteria for presentations. Finalise facilities.

10 Conduct presentations and evaluation.

11 Advise unsuccessful bidders and give them the opportunity to hear the reasons why they were not chosen.

12 Negotiate final details with the successful bidder.

13 Arrange an initial meeting to detail the plan and to get the project under way.

6
■ ■ ■

Evaluating the consultant's proposals and agreeing terms

The objectives for this chapter are as follows:

- to enable you to evaluate a consultant's proposal in an objective manner;

- to explain what you should expect in the way of documents, reports, presentations and other deliverable items;

- to enable you to assess the consultant's style and size and determine their appropriateness to the project and the client;

- to describe how to test what the consultant is going to do and what is required of you as the client;

- to explain the various approaches and methodologies that a consultant may intend to adopt, and to help you to determine their relevance to your objectives;

- to enable you to appreciate the consultant's project management approach and its implications for the proposed timetable;

- to explain the various ways in which the fees may be structured – in particular, with relation to expenses and other additional costs;

- to explain the importance of references and describe the sorts of questions that should be asked when taking them up;

- to introduce other issues, such as intellectual property rights and non-disclosure of confidential information.

Evaluation criteria

■ ■ ■

Before the final submission deadline for proposals, you need to finalise and document the evaluation criteria and method, so that everyone can be clear that the process is fair. Doing this will provide a fully auditable process which then can be reviewed and shown to have been above board. This is especially important for those organisations in the public sector who are subject to strict procurement regulations, and those companies and other agencies who have strict standing instructions with which they have to be able to demonstrate compliance. For everybody else it is simply good practice.

Appendix F is an example of a formal approach to evaluation that minimises the effect of persuasive salespeople or non-essential gloss in a proposal. However, this approach does require the criteria to be predefined.

For all but the smallest project the evaluation criteria will be on several levels. I always start by breaking the issues that need to be assessed into a group of high-level headings, say:

- the bidding company;

- the bidder's understanding;

- approach and methodology;

- client involvement;

- the consultancy firm's team;

- relevant experience;

- accreditations, references, etc;

- cost.

I then break down each heading into a series of sub-headings. For example, 'company' might break down to:

- initial contacts;

- financial standing;

- culture and compatibility;

- responsiveness.

If necessary I break each sub-heading down further, until I reach a level of detail that is appropriate and that matches the structure of the format required for the proposal as conveniently as possible. For large selection processes I have taken it down to five or six levels. A more complete breakdown is included as an example in Appendix F. A computerised spreadsheet becomes obligatory by that stage and is a recommended tool for most evaluations.

Weights have to be applied to each item; how to do this is described in Appendix F. These are at each level, and scoring, usually from 0 (no compliance) to 10 (full compliance), is done at each item that has not been broken down further. The scores have the weights applied and they ripple up through the levels, applying weights at each level. The result is a final score; the bidder with the highest score is the one selected.

You may be tempted to fiddle with the evaluation model if your instinctive choice does not have the highest score. Avoid this temptation: if you alter the criteria, or even alter just the weights, at that point then you will undermine the whole process. You will lose the ability to demonstrate strict compliance with your corporate governance rules and you will leave yourself open to being swayed by subjective judgements, a persuasive salesperson or other emotional responses. That is exactly what you were trying to avoid.

Initial contacts
■ ■ ■

As has already been said, you should include all contacts with the prospective adviser as part of the selection process. As a consultant I certainly work on that basis. There are some simple tests one can apply. Does the consultant respond speedily and effectively to requests for information? Do they return calls? Are they on time with proposals? Do they make it easy for you to buy from them?

The market is sufficiently competitive in most fields that you do not have to use slow or surly advisers. If they cannot deliver what they promise when they are trying to sell to you they certainly will not meet project deadlines. If they fail at this stage do not use them.

This is a case of 'do as I do as well as I say'. Only in the most exceptional circumstances does a supplier get a second chance to sell me their products if they have failed to return my call or send me promised information. I find somebody who *wants* my business.

Consultant's proposal
■ ■ ■

First impressions are important. If the proposal did not arrive on time and the consultant has failed the first test then, as a general rule, I would suggest that that proposal should not be considered further and the consultant should be immediately ruled out. If they cannot meet a reasonable deadline for the production of a proposal for new work, then can you expect them to meet project deadlines in the future? In formal procurement processes the rules make clear that no proposal that arrives after the deadline will be considered. This is especially true in the public sector and it is my experience that this rule is followed to the letter.

Next, you should consider the overall presentation of the proposal. Is it attractively presented and laid out clearly? With the availability of inexpensive computers and printers, even the smallest consultancy firm should be able to produce a neat and tidy document. Knowledge-based workers, such as professional advisers and consultants, do not have tangible products except for their reports; it is reasonable therefore to pay attention to the detail of their presentation.

Some very capable consultants, especially technical specialists, regard attention to presentation as superficial gloss, and see the content as all-important. They are, in my view, mistaken. It is often said that we eat with our eyes and that an attractively presented meal puts us in the right frame of mind to enjoy its taste. The same is true of an attractively presented proposal or report – we want to find out what it has to say. The converse is also true; an unattractive document tells the reader that the writer does not consider it important, so they probably do not need to read it. As a result the message is lost.

You also need to consider whether the size of the proposal is commensurate with the scale and complexity of the proposed project. Some consultancies seem to think that a client is going to weigh the proposals and choose the heaviest! I have seen proposals for projects of under £30,000 which run to nearly two hundred pages. If the consultant cannot get their own message across in a concise way, what chance do they have of producing a report that simplifies your problem and makes the recommendations clear? At the Ford Motor Company it is a general rule that no report to senior management is more than one page in length. This is true even where the implications of the recommendations in the report may cost the company millions of dollars. The argument is that if a manager has been asked to make a recommendation that is what they should do, and they should be able to summarise it in one page. If there is a need to re-examine the recommendation or to audit the choice, then the one-page report is backed up by the working file which contains all the documents and working papers used in preparing the recommendation. The same should be true for consultants.

In your document inviting proposals you will have requested a particular structure for all proposals. Has the consultant followed that instruction in their proposal? (It is permissible, of course, to add additional supporting material as appendices or in additional sections at the end of the requested submission.) If they have not followed that most basic of instruction, then again you should score them down heavily; it is your decision as to whether they should be excluded. Ignoring instructions should ring warning bells about a consultant's quality assurance procedures and about their ability to follow clear guidance.

Proposals can come in a variety of formats, especially when a more informal selection process is being used. I have won work with proposals as short as two pages. The length is unimportant providing it contains the details that the client requires. A more typical example is the engagement letter in Appendix C. (Please bear in mind that this has had additional sections added for illustration.) This serves initially as a proposal and, when the terms have been agreed, it has the final acceptance section added below the signature and then forms the contract.

Even though the letter is brief, it still contains all the essential sections:

- objectives, which in this case also contain the background to the project;

- how the consultant will approach the work;

- the responsibilities of both consultant and client;

- fees and payment terms;

- the staff who will work on the project;

- timescale; the required completion date is in the objectives;

- deliverables are listed in the 'Our role' section as the responsibility of the consultant.

Brevity is possible and to be recommended. It may take longer to write concisely but it shows respect for the reader's time.

Even if you have not formally requested one in your invitation there should be a brief, probably one page, summary of the proposal. This should include the total proposed cost of the project. The lack of such a summary, even when not specifically requested, shows a certain lack of either experience or professionalism. As a matter of course, all consultancy reports should include a brief executive summary so that a busy reader can understand the essence of the report without having to read the full document.

153

As you read the report for the first time, consider the accessibility of the language. Is the proposal full of jargon? Is it likely to be understood by the intended audience? Some jargon may be acceptable, but only if the same jargon is used by the client group commissioning the consultant. You have to consider whether you will be able to understand the consultants' reports and recommendations. I would suggest that you do not compromise on this point, as this is a major problem with consultants in general and it will only change if clients insist on it doing so. Here is your chance to make a stand for all clients!

As part of the same process you should consider the clarity of the proposal. Have the consultants tried to conceal or bury essential points in the text? This is particularly common with items such as expenses or restrictions on the promises that may be made in the document. Look for them. If they are hidden, score the proposal down on the clarity criteria.

Consultant's tip

Proposal writers (not just consultants) use all sorts of tricks that are an insult to the intelligence of the customer. Look out for a couple of them in particular:

■ Not totalling the costs. Some consultants just list the elements that make up the total bill but do not add them up, as if you will not get out a calculator and do so.

■ Creating a false impression of accuracy by coming up with a price that is apparently calculated to the last penny. We all know that you cannot be that precise on a consultancy bid. On even a small project a consultant would be very lucky to get the total of the time, travel, administrative costs and other expenses accurate closer than to the nearest £100. I would ignore any spurious claimed accuracy to within less than 5%. The fees in a proposal for services are a guess and guesses cannot be accurate except by luck.

Treat such silly games with the contempt they deserve. Score down the proposal.

The final assessment of the general impressions of the proposal should consider the spelling, punctuation and other attention to detail. With modern word-processors there is no excuse for misspelled words. Of course spell checkers do not detect words used in the wrong context, that is down to proof reading by the authors and their colleagues. Bear in mind that if the consultants are sloppy in their proof reading of a sales proposal then they are likely to be sloppy in the production of their reports. You should question whether they would be equally sloppy in the rest of their work.

Remember that in most cases the proposal will form part of the contract, so any areas of dispute or that are not understood should be resolved before acceptance. All such clarification and explanation should be in writing, as it should be an addendum to the proposal unless the proposal itself is amended to include the necessary changes.

Consultancy style, size and location

■ ■ ■

Style and size

The style of the consultancy must match that of the client. Whilst the compatibility of cultures was a key factor in preparing the short list to be invited to bid for the work, now is the time to review their formal responses for cultural compatibility. Of course those that reach the final stage have to demonstrate their ability to share the client's values at presentation, during the discussion of their proposal and even during the final negotiations of the contract.

155

There are broadly five types of consultancy firm: first there are the very large firms with large international networks and fee rates to match. There is no doubt that such firms have the resources to undertake almost any project anywhere in the world, but they are not usually interested in smaller projects unless they are for a client who may offer more substantial projects in the future.

There is then a second tier of firms that see themselves as offering a similar service to the 'big boys' and at rates not much lower. Some can compete in their strong specialities, and indeed may be the foremost authorities in some. But they usually do not have the breadth of expertise or the depth of the big players.

Next there are the 'boutique' operations, which have often been formed from specialist groups within much larger firms. In their particular field of expertise they should be leading players, but they do not have the spread to take on all types of project. They may not be able to accept the big, multi-disciplinary projects that cross many functions; nor would they seek to under normal circumstances. They are specialist players in niche markets, and often command high fees on a par with the biggest firms.

Fourthly, there are small firms, which cover the spectrum from leading experts to the incompetent. Their fees do not necessarily coincide with their competence. Most will do a good job within that which they know and understand. Some will have chosen consultancy, some will be in it because of circumstances such as redundancy. Some of the latter will take to the work and prosper; many, unfortunately, will fall by the wayside. Generally fees will be a little lower at this end of the market, and in some cases, ridiculously low from people who are not seeking to make consultancy a career. Be suspicious of very low fees, a matter we will discuss in more detail later.

The final group of firms consists of formal networks of independent consultants. Many are franchises and are supported by a levy on members – some of the big firms started as loose networks of independent firms, which over time coalesced into national and then international firms. A few of these groups, unfortunately, seem only interested in taking redundancy cheques from people in return for training in 'how to be a consultant'. As we explained earlier, being a consultant means more than having some good technical skills; it is not a skill that can be taught in a few days, or even weeks.

The idea behind a network of consultants is to give independent consultants some of the strengths of the larger practice. The better networks offer things like peer support, access to libraries and other specialists, and, perhaps the biggest attraction, marketing skills and muscle. This is an area where the new consultant often feels most need for support. Some have worked well for many years, but in the recent past several networks have broken up in acrimony, often about unfair sharing of business generated by the network.

I would argue that the size of the consultancy is not an important factor, as long as it is big enough to cope with the project. (But then I run a smallish consultancy.) The most important thing is that a consultancy has the right people available to do the work. However, there are times when the size of the firm, or at least of its network, *is* important. Some projects require a wide spread of specialist expertise or an international network. In such cases a large practice may be most appropriate, but do bear in mind that many smaller or national practices may have wide formal and informal networks. In such cases the small practice may be able to deliver the same quality across a wide range of skills even on an international basis.

At the time of writing I am working with a Texas-based consultancy on developing a joint approach to the US market. I have never actually met my contact face to face; our relationship has been developed entirely through electronic mail. Through such mediums as CompuServe and the Internet I have access to experts in most spheres, and it does not matter where they are located. Knowledge is easily shared electronically.

157

Location

Many clients worry about the base location of a consultancy practice. On the other hand, consultants tend not to worry about the location of their clients as they are used to travelling extensively in their work. It matters little where a consultant lives. For most projects a consultancy will organise themselves in such a way that they can service the project effectively.

All that notwithstanding, there are projects where the location of the consultant does matter. Typically these are where the consultant needs frequent short meetings with the client. Such projects are relatively unusual, as most benefit from the consultant giving a substantial block of time, say a week, or a day or two a week, to the project, in which case they can stay over. The amount of travelling then becomes less significant.

Consultant's tip

The leading individual on a consultant's project team will usually set its style, quality and performance. This may be materially different from that of the consultancy firm itself.

Buy on the basis of the person, not the firm.

Objectives/deliverables

The proposal should clearly state what the consultant is going to deliver in the way of reports presentations, etc., and what the project will achieve for the client. Achievements should be stated in measurable terms. As part of your assessment of the proposal these deliverables should be paired with objectives described in the invitation to tender document. They should also be compared to the other aims that have been included in the evaluation criteria, some of which may be in the form of aspirations rather than required objectives. These should be included in the evaluation criteria, but with lower waiting than the required items.

I have already warned about standard solutions wrapped up as consultancy 'products'. Do not use a firm of advisers to analyse your problem if they talk about their product for your industry, problem or whatever. If you do you should not be surprised if the recommended solution looks remarkably like their 'product'. This is a growing danger with many consultancy firms, particularly the big ones, who are moving into providing information systems development, facilities management and support for 'outsourced' functions. They claim that there is separation between such elements and the consultancy arm, but you have to be aware of the possibilities and form your own judgement of how complete that separation will be when the firm comes under fee pressure.

Above all, buy the benefits, not the work to be done. The work is only a means to an end.

Consultant's and client's roles

■ ■ ■

The bidder should set out what they see as the respective responsibilities of the client and consultant. Examine these carefully, as they may well have implications for the total cost of the project.

If the consultant is adopting an approach that requires the client's staff to do more of the work, then this should achieve more knowledge transfer, but there will be a cost to the client in terms of making their people available.

Similarly, if the consultant is suggesting that the client should be responsible for travel costs, such as aeroplane and rail tickets or hotels, then these need to be quantified as part of the cost. They will probably not be in the proposal.

159

Equally importantly, you must decide whether you can take on the responsibilities suggested in the proposal. If you do not feel that you have the necessary resources then you need to consider whether the consultant has misinterpreted your capability or desires from the invitation to tender documents and related discussions. Alternatively, are they perhaps a bit stretched themselves as far as resources or skills are concerned? Perhaps the consultants are getting a bit out of their depth with this bid.

Check that the role the bidder is proposing for themselves fits with the role and responsibilities you wish to place on them. However, do not expect the consultant to take over the management of your business – any consultant who proposes that they should does not understand what consultancy is all about.

Approach and methodology

■ ■ ■

One section of the proposal should contain broad details of how the consultant will approach the work and should outline the methods and tools that they will use. Do not expect to get an instruction manual as to how to undertake the work yourself. You should not expect the consultant to give a detailed step-by-step explanation of how they are going to approach the project. Nor should you expect them to include all their questionnaires, interview structures, presentation material or other documents. Such material is commercially confidential and you should not expect to get all such material for free. If you did you could then go away and do the work yourself using the consultants' expensively prepared material. It may also be impossible to plan ahead with this level of detail. Few projects go exactly to plan; the approach has to be modified in the light of the findings, so a lot of the working documents will be prepared as they are needed on the basis of what has already been discovered.

160 In some consultancy specialisms it is usual to undertake fairly detailed preparatory work. This is particularly true in fields such as advertising, public relations and in the creative fields such as design. In such cases the consultants may be required, and expect, to come up with some broad concepts with regard to the project. In these cases it is impossible to be definitive about what should and should not be included in a proposal as far as approach and methods, or indeed ideas, are concerned.

The scale of the project will also have considerable impact on what should be included in the proposal. It would be unreasonable to expect a proposal for a small, say £5,000, project to have as extensive a description of the approach to be used as one for a £500,000 project. Remember that preparing a proposal is expensive. If the cost of preparation is out of proportion to the value of the possible project, then consultants will not bid.

Timetable

■ ■ ■

Although many invitations to tender for consultancy projects ask for a detailed project plan, generally I believe this to be inappropriate and impractical. However, there should be a reasonably comprehensive plan giving the expected overall phasing of the work, the main reporting and decision points and the time commitment required by the client.

The detailed plan, in my view, can only be produced once the final terms of reference have been agreed with the selected adviser. In my experience these can often be very different from those proposed by the client, or indeed incorporated in the proposal by the bidder. If the process is working well (with lots of communication), by the time the contracts are signed both parties will have learnt considerably more about the proposed work, and this should be reflected in the contracted terms of reference.

Project management

■ ■ ■

Under this heading a bidder needs to be able to explain their approach to project management. What reporting will be used internally and with the client project manager? Will there be regular, brief, progress meetings between project managers? Or is a bureaucratic approach being proposed, with lots of minutes, activity reports, time-sheets and other documents being passed backwards and forwards? A balance has to be struck; some paperwork is required but, as discussed elsewhere, it is very easy for a consultant to generate the appearance of being busy and making progress out of all proportion to the truth.

All you can really look for with regard to formal project management is whether the bidder has formal project management systems and software that they use routinely. If you have requested a particular approach or software for project reporting, such as PRINCE, has the bidder claimed experience of it and/or a willingness to adopt it for this project?

The key to project management is a focus on results and achievement of tangible objectives. Recording of inputs is often self-justification and covering one's back rather than genuine management.

Personnel to be used

■ ■ ■

The proposal should include the names and expertise of the key personnel to be used on the project. It should also give a feel for the amount of involvement each consultant will have. Discount any people, especially senior staff, who are included with little or no time commitment; they are there to make the bid look credible, and you may not see them again after the presentation.

Bear in mind that there may be other specialists who will be used to support the main team. They may appear to undertake a particular, usually technical, review and may report their findings to the main consultancy team for inclusion in their analysis. This is usual with larger projects and it would be unreasonable to expect all such individuals to be listed in the proposal – the bidder would have to list almost everybody because they could never be sure who might be needed as the project unfolds.

Make sure that you meet the key members of the consultant's team who will be working on your project. By that I do not simply mean the most senior staff; rather ensure that you meet those who are actually going to do much of the work – they may be quite junior in rank. An earlier tip was that you should choose the managing consultant and buy the person not the firm. The same is true to a lesser extent for all the main members of the team. Ideally they should be at the presentation, but if the team is very large that this may be too unwieldy and inappropriate. In this case arrange for all team members to be introduced at an early stage, and make it clear that if they do not fit with the ethos of your organisation it may be necessary for someone else to be used.

The proposal should include an outline curriculum vitae for each member of the proposed team in an appendix to the main document. Typically each CV should be about a page long and should be tailored to highlight experience relevant to the proposed work. Look for the length of experience of the consultant, how long they have been in consultancy and to what extent their experience is in consultancy or industry management. As we have discussed earlier, managers and consultants are different and need different skills. Will each member of the bidder's team be able to bring something to *your* project?

Consultant's tip

Choose someone you like, with whom you are comfortable, and who is enthusiastic and fun. You are likely to spend quite a lot of time together, possibly in stressful situations. You need be able to laugh together at the absurdity of the situation if your world is collapsing around your heads.

If you choose someone who is enthusiastic and fun, they will create a lively climate in which things get done.

163

Presentation

■ ■ ■

The presentation should be strictly limited to a length and format advised to the participating bidders in advance. Typically it should be between sixty and ninety minutes long, with usually twenty to thirty minutes of this time given over to the consultant's presentation. The rest of the time should be used for questions or discussion. If the consultants take longer over the presentation than agreed you should mark them down, unless this is due to interruptions from the assessment panel.

If the consultant team is properly prepared they will anticipate the more obvious questions and answer them in the presentation. When it comes to asking questions the selection team should direct some to all members, including the most junior, of the consultant's team, not just the leader. Also, when asking general questions related to a technical area, ask them of someone of a different specialism, to see if they have a feel for the cross-functional issues. The individual may not be able to answer the question, but they should be able to make a sensible comment and pass it on to the right person. If they can do so without obvious discomfort it probably shows maturity and confidence which will be reflected in the way they handle such issues in the project. Alternatively it may show that they have been well groomed. Either case shows professionalism.

Listen to what the consultants say about you, the client, and your project, rather than what they say about themselves. You know how big they are and their reputation because you have done your homework, so if they reiterate all that they are not respecting your professionalism, or they are padding. Similarly, if they talk a lot about what they have done for others, they are not focusing on what is most important for the presentation – what they can do for you.

What you really want from a firm of advisers is to be surprised in a positive way, causing you to say, 'Why didn't we think of that?'. If this happens they are showing not only their ability to be creative but also that they have understood the issues well enough to be confident in such ideas. You will have to judge whether such confidence is well founded. If it is, then you are probably well on the way to finding a suitable consultant. Ideally they should produce ideas and issues that the other bidders have missed.

Bearing in mind what has just been said, watch out for consultancies that field the ace sales team at the presentation. You should require in your invitation to bid that the team making the presentation are those in the proposal who will actually be doing your work. Be suspicious if there are any apparently key personnel missing from the presentation.

The consultants' team will have rehearsed the presentation in front of colleagues and it almost certainly will have been honed. So be suspicious of a poor presentation – it may indicate lack of preparation or lack of understanding of the client's business or the project under discussion. It may be the first and last opportunity some of the selection committee will have to meet the advisers before the work is awarded, so it should give an insight into the professionalism of the consultants.

Quality
■ ■ ■

What does the bidder have to say about their quality control procedures? Even a small firm or a sole trader should have proper procedures in place for quality control. I have a reciprocal arrangement with another firm for peer review of our work. This is simple to set up and operate and is of mutual benefit. There is therefore no excuse for inadequate quality control.

165

References
■ ■ ■

My first piece of advice is always to ask for references and always to take them up. Consultants and professional advisers are jealous of their reputations, which are hard won and easily lost. They should be willing and ready to provide references. However, such consultants will also be very strict about client confidentiality so will not, usually, give references out without first speaking with their client contact to check that it is acceptable to do so. This is also a matter of basic courtesy, so do not expect referees to be supplied instantly. Sometimes a consultant will be able to do so because they have a standing arrangement, but even in such cases I prefer to speak to the referee first. In any case, I usually prefer to choose a client for whom I have done similar work or, if that is not possible, that is in a similar industry to the prospective client. That way the reference is more valuable to the prospective client.

I would advise calling the referee on the telephone; they are likely to be more candid than in writing. Telephoning is also less time-consuming for the referee, and you are likely to get some free advice on how to make the best of the proposed firm.

Some of the questions that you should ask of a referee about any professional adviser include the following:

- What did you use them for and when?

- Would you use them again? And have you?

- What did they achieve?

- How do they compare with others you have used?

- Did they fit in? Were they sensitive to the culture of the organisation?

- Did they meet their time and budget targets?

- What are their strengths and weaknesses?

- How did you choose them?

- Did they meet project objectives?

Clearly there are many more questions that can and should be asked. No doubt some questions will arise from the answers to others. Document both what is said by the referee and, equally importantly, how it was said. You may need to read between the lines.

Fees and payment terms
■ ■ ■

The fees charged by consultants vary widely between firms and individuals. Typically the highest could be ten times the lowest. The ratio may be greater in some cases. The basis on which they charge is also variable and can include the following:

- day rate or hourly basis for work done;

- retainer to make themselves available to the client as required;

- fixed price for a piece of work;
- contingent fees based on the benefits achieved for the client.

Although most advisers have a scale rate which will be charged for routine work, the actual fee rate in the proposal will be influenced by a variety of factors, including the following:

- market conditions and competition;
- the firm's standing;
- the assignment;
- the risk;
- the benefits to the client;
- market rates;
- how much the consultant wants the client;
- what the client can afford.

The advisory firm's schedule of rates is rarely fixed and in practice only provides a guideline for routine work. It will be used as a basis for costing up a proposal, but then a view will be taken as to the likely competition, the nature of the work and whether the project might be a precursor to further work for the client. The price will then be adjusted, up or down, to a figure that the bidder feels is right for this particular project.

The fees may be increased because the benefits to the client will be substantial or because the nature of the work is such that there will be little competition. They may be raised because the consultant does not really want to do the work but needs to submit a proposal so as to be invited to bid for future work.

Reasons for reducing fees from scale rates are numerous and include the obvious ones such as the consultant needing the work, the client having limited resources or the market sector demanding it. There may be another reason for the consultant to bid low. It may be that the project is seen as a 'Trojan horse';

it is a way to win the client so that the consultancy firm is more likely to win future, more valuable, work from them. This loss-leader approach can work against the consultant, because the client may expect the same level of fees for future work which may not be profitable for the consultant.

Consultants also bid low when they want the project to strengthen their references or to get a reference site in a new business sector. They may have an approach that has worked well for one industry and which they want to apply elsewhere. Without the specialist knowledge of the industry they will have difficulty, so they bid for work and pitch the price as low as possible to help them to gain that opportunity. When I worked for a larger firm we sometimes worked in new markets simply for expenses, sometimes less, to gain credibility in the target industry.

168 In the case of the small independent they may bid low because they can afford to since their costs are low. It may also be because their expectations for salaries are low for a variety of reasons. They may have been middle managers on modest salaries who do not need or expect to be high earners. It may be because they do not believe in high salaries for political or other reasons.

It must be said that many start-up and independent consultants pitch their prices low because they do not really understand the costs of being a consultant. Most people running their own genuine consultancies, doing all their own marketing and so on, are pushed to bill, on average, more than 1,000 chargeable hours per year. That is about half of a working year – the rest is spent on finding new clients, on personal development, administration and the like. It does not seem to matter what the specialism is, or even where in the world the firm is based, about a thousand hours is the limit. Also, personal development, research and training are expensive in both time and money. It is no surprise therefore that few new consultancy firms last more than two years.

There is also another common and somewhat sad reason for low fees. It is a result of the increase in redundancy amongst middle managers and technical specialists. Many are desperate to earn something to pay the mortgage or whatever and see consultancy as a relatively easy option. Unfortunately it is not, as it requires rather more than technical skills. As well as the skills needed to perform consultancy well there are the marketing skills. Few of those who are made redundant or who retire early have that experience and it is expensive and time-consuming to learn, hence the high failure rate of new practices. Such consultancies often bid low in their desperation to get work and hence offer unrealistically low rates. What they do not realise is that, very often, high(ish) fees are needed to give the client comfort and a feeling of value. It is like perfume – high prices are needed to give credibility to the product.

Consultant's Casebook

BE CAREFUL ABOUT FIXED RATES

Fixed prices or fixed rates are not always the answer for the client. For example, a consultant agreed fixed day rates for the life of a computer systems project. The work was expected to take a few months, a year at the most, to specify, select, purchase and implement the new computer system. The consultant was therefore happy to agree the capped rates for the duration of the project. The client thought they were getting security and protection against rising prices at a time of inflation.

Unfortunately the client took rather longer than expected, due to their own internal reasons, not any failure by the consultant. After five years they had still not made their selection let alone completed the implementation. The period of high inflation meant that the consultant was by then working for this client at half their current charge-out rate. As might be appreciated, the consultant found their motivation to work on this project suffered, as did the quality of their work. Consequently the client did not get value for money either.

The moral of this tale is that either party could, and should, have identified the problem and agreed new terms or, more probably, shelved the original project. They could then have returned to

▶

▶

the work as a new project at a time when the client was able to take it forward at a sensible pace.

The consultant has a responsibility to ensure that the client is getting value for money. In this case they were not, due to no fault of the consultant (in the beginning at any rate). Even so, the consultant should have pointed out the problems to the client and suggested a suspension of the work. By agreeing to such a pause, even if the fee rates were increased when the work restarted, the client would almost certainly have spent less in real terms over the life of the project. When a project runs this slowly the client is wasting a lot of time and money.

Consultant's tip

There is a saying amongst consultants that advice is worth what you pay for it!

Free advice is not valued, and I have seen excellent grant-aided consultancy advice ignored because it had not cost the client enough: they could afford to ignore it. If they had paid the full price (which was still low in consultancy terms) they would have given the advice more attention, because the money was coming out of their own pocket. That is the principal reason I try to avoid grant-aided projects.

I am not advising buying at the highest price and I would certainly recommend that you do not simply buy on price. Look at the value for money the consultant is offering. Do the benefits justify the cost? If they do then the adviser is offering value for money. Choose the consultant who is offering the best value for money and with whom you can work.

Fixed price

Increasingly, consultants are working to a fixed price for project-based work; in other words, for work that has a clear beginning and end. Fixed prices are not appropriate to an ongoing advisory role, although a fixed day rate may be agreed, with, typically, an annual review of the rate.

Fixed prices may or may not include expenses. This depends on the nature of the work and the predictability of costs. If they can be predicted they should be included.

It is probable that a bid at a fixed price and an estimate on the basis of time and materials for the same work by the same consultant will be different. The fixed-rate price will be higher than the estimate because the consultant is taking on the risk that the work will take longer. They have to build in a contingency margin. With the day rate estimate the *client* should build in a margin for overrun, because they are taking the risk. The more uncertain the details of the work, the bigger a safety margin has to be allowed. Only you, the client, can judge which is right for you.

171

Contingent fees

Whilst results-based fees are slowly becoming more general they are difficult for all concerned. One of the big problems is agreeing measures of success on which to base fees that are closely related to the performance of the consultant. Most measures in business are heavily influenced by other factors, both internal and external to the client. If sales increase is this due to the advice of a marketing consultant or just a general improvement in market conditions?

As a result both clients and consultants are uncomfortable with fees contingent on performance. Clients can resent what they see as windfall profits for the consultants from other work done by themselves. Consultants worry about clients not carrying through their recommendations effectively.

I would suggest that unless you have considerable experience of using external advisers and tight in-house management you avoid results-based fees. Even if you do have such experience, think long and hard about how performance improvements are measured and how well they can be tied to the consultant's advice. Then think again – will you be comfortable paying very much higher fees (over other bases) if the results are better than expected?

Day rate/time and materials

Traditionally most professional advisers have been paid for their time at some agreed rate, with expenses and other costs passed on to the client. This is still the most common method for any general advisory work that may be ongoing or requested on an as-needed basis.

For project-based work the trend is strongly towards fixed prices, but bear in mind that any additional work not covered by the terms of reference will be charged over and above the agreed fee. You should be given the option of having the work done or not, and the fee basis should be formally agreed in advance.

My recent experience is that nearly all invitations to tender for project consultancy require fixed prices and often demand that all expenses be included in the price.

Delays and changes

Anybody who has ever had any serious building work done will be only too aware of the cost of changing the specification during the work. The same is true with professional advice: changing the scope or nature of the work is likely to mean that the consultant, quite properly, will seek extra fees. This is why so much emphasis was placed on both the project definition stages and the subsequent discussions with the adviser before agreeing the terms of reference.

With some projects changes will be needed in the light of initial findings, but these can often be anticipated and the terms of reference designed around them. By doing so the client and consultant can agree a contingency element to cover increased costs or, even better, treat the proposal as a two-stage project. The first stage is an initial analysis to determine the proper scope and size of the main body of the work; the terms of reference and fees for the main work are agreed after the first stage is complete. This gives the client the opportunity, before it is too late, to reconfigure workload to take more of the work in-house if professional fees have to be reduced.

Delays to the project caused by the client are likely to increase the amount of time the consultant has to give to the work. In such cases the consultant should advise the client of the financial implications of their failure to perform and agree to explore how the delay can be resolved.

Advisers should always tell a client if costs are rising above the estimate in the terms of reference. They should not simply drop an unexpectedly high bill on the client. If you follow the advice in this book you will talk to the consultants frequently and there will be no surprises.

173

Expenses

With many consultancy projects there are expenses incurred by the consultants. What is and is not included should be clearly stated in the proposal and should be built into the final engagement letter or contract. It is common practice to ✓ charge all travelling costs, including those from the consultant's base to the client's office. Many would argue that these should be built into the price, and this is something I have done for many years. However, there may be exceptional costs; for instance I sometimes have to visit potential or current suppliers on behalf of the client. In such cases, where the expense is not easily predicted at the start of the project, I include details of the circumstances under which I will charge and the basis I will use. Generally, train or air fares, hotel and subsistence are charged at cost, and travel by car at an agreed rate. In the latter case I usually try to use the same scale charge that the client uses for staff using their own cars (as in the example in Appendix C).

As the people paying the bills, clients should make it clear what they will cover in the way of subsistence expenses. For example, an evening meal and perhaps a half bottle of wine, but not a serious drinking session. Similarly, the consultant should use the type of hotels, flight or rail travel class that would be provided by the client to its senior staff and directors. A sensitive consultant will accept this, as it is an area which can hurt the consultant's standing with the client's staff, with whom they have to work. If the consultant wants to go upmarket then they should bear the difference in cost and be aware of the other dangers.

Some advisers charge what I regard as routine administrative costs to the client. These might include telephone call charges, photocopying, secretarial support, delivery charges and other incidental costs. Whilst there is custom and practice in different parts of the advisory industry, generally I feel that these costs should be carried by the basic fee rate. However, one can envisage projects where these items could be major expenses, for instance printing a large number of copies of a document, or telephoning or using a courier to deliver documents to a director on holiday abroad. Such items should be easily identified as exceptional and would not include routine telephone calls between client and consultant or the making of ten copies of the final report for discussion. These latter items can, and should, be included in the basic price.

174

Where travel, hotel and other costs cannot be included in the price you, the client, should consider picking these up directly. Of course it means that you will have the administrative burden, but you can keep control of the level of such expenses. Some advisers seek to add an administrative surcharge to expenses of 5–15%. In such cases you should certainly pick up the costs directly.

Payment terms

Payment terms can be very varied. Most consultants bill time and materials at the end of each month, with payment due within 30 days. It is not uncommon amongst the professions for payment to be due on presentation of the bill – I have certainly seen such terms on both accountants' and solicitors' invoices. However, payment within 30 days is more usual.

If the work is phased the bill may be presented as each stage is completed. Certainly if the project is short, say up to ten days or so, then I would expect the bill to be presented on completion. The billing on longer projects, especially if phased, should be such that the last bill should not be raised until after the work is completed. Payment would then be on usual commercial terms agreed in advance.

Some consultants bill the first month's work as soon as they start, with thirty-day payment terms so that payment falls due as the first month's work is completed. Such consultants argue that they are not then working a month in hand and if the client is slow in paying the work can be paused until payment is received without exposing the consultant to further risk. This is not common and I would expect most clients to resist such a basis, unless there is a particularly high risk of them not meeting their commitments. If there is such a risk, payment should be made in advance or be guaranteed in some other way.

Other issues
■ ■ ■

As a result of nearly twenty years' experience of consultancy and project implementation I am certain that the major reasons for failure, or only partial success, of projects are neither technical nor technological problems. More often than not such failures arise from not having addressed the people issues. Usually the users have not been involved or have been allowed to stand outside the project.

People may not be able to make a bad solution work, but they can certainly stop a good technical solution from being effective. Actually, if one can get staff to believe in the changes they will often make a less than ideal solution work remarkably well. If users believe that a solution is unworkable they will ensure that their belief is realised.

Executive summary

We have stressed the importance of demonstrating fair and open procurement, so it is essential that you prepare the evaluation criteria and method before receiving any proposals, or in any case before the presentation. Only if this is done can bidders and auditors be reassured that the assessment rules are not designed to favour a particular bid.

Evaluation has to cover a wide range of issues, from appropriate financial viability of the bidder to their competence and experience. There are also many subjective decisions to be made, such as whether the proposer's style is compatible with that of the client organisation. This also needs to go down to the level of individuals, for example to confirm that the client's project manager is able to develop an effective working relationship with the lead consultant. Ideally they should like each other and enjoy each other's company, especially if the project is going to be a long one. These judgements, whilst subjective, need to be scored and incorporated into the evaluation framework in as objective a manner as possible, so that they are given due importance and are not unduly influenced by a particularly successful meeting or whatever. Hence the need for preparation of evaluation criteria in advance.

Although there are a couple of major evaluation points of proposal and presentation, the evaluation has a continuous element that runs from the initial long list through all contact with potential suppliers of the service, however informal, until the contract is awarded.

Proposals should be clear and should strictly comply with the requirements set out in the invitation. They should also be appropriate in size and content to the scale and nature of the project. They should clearly set out what responsibility the consultant will take and what is expected of the client, both in terms of facilities and time commitment by staff. The main consultants who will be working on the project should be listed and the scale of their involvement detailed. There should be no one listed who does not have a clear role and involvement with the proposed work – if there is, and it is a senior person, they should be ignored as they are there simply to add credibility to the bid.

The presentation should also be prepared with a clear format and a timetable that is closely followed. Assessment should be as for the proposal and should be incorporated into the same, or similar, evaluation model.

Consultants and professional advisers take their reputations seriously and should be willing and able to provide references. They may not be willing to do so without speaking to the referees first, because of client confidentiality issues and common courtesy. References should be provided, and checked, before the contract is awarded since if they are not satisfactory you may wish to reconsider your choice of consultant.

Fees are a matter of considerable contention, but generally clients should seek fixed prices, including all but the most exceptional expenses, for project-based work that has a clear start and finish (hence the importance of measurable objectives). For other general *ad hoc* advice, a time-based price should be agreed and again all routine expenses should be included.

Remember that very different prices can be quoted for the same terms of reference by the same consultant. They will depend on how thorough and wide-ranging the work has to be. You need to recognise when the consultant is proposing a relatively superficial analysis to keep the price low. Conversely you also need to spot consultants padding the job with unnecessarily detailed work to increase the fees. This emphasises the importance of the definition of the problem, SMART objectives and, above all, the value of competitive tendering.

Finally, ensure that the consultant has demonstrated an

understanding of the people issues – more projects fail for this reason than because of failure of technology.

Checklist

1 Make sure the evaluation criteria are defined and the method to be used is agreed. Check that it is easy to score and get a clear result. Ask whether it gives due priority to the essential over the desirable.

2 Use all contact with the prospective adviser as part of evaluation.

3 Consider the proposal:

   – Did it arrive on time and packaged as requested?

   – Is it appropriate in size and well presented?

   – Is the language clear and accurate in all aspects – spelling, grammar, etc?

   – Is it complete and does it follow the requested format?

4 Is the style and culture of the bidding firm compatible with your own?

5 Can you accommodate the role proposed for you by the consultant?

6 Are you happy with the consultant's role?

7 Do you understand and agree with the approach the consultant is proposing to adopt for this project? Is the emphasis compatible with your required objectives?

8 Will the timetable meet your requirements and are you confident that the consultant has the ability to manage and deliver the project to time and cost? Is their project management heavily paper-based with activity reports, contact reports, progress meetings and minutes? If so, is this a smokescreen for lack of experience or ability?

9 Are the people in the proposal suitably experienced and will they be able to give the project the commitment that

it will need? Are there senior people in the bid just to add weight with no real time involvement on the project?

10 At the presentation, seek to dig deeper into these issues and especially into the compatibility of cultures and personalities.

11 Take up references and assess whether they are good, satisfactory or indifferent. Use the telephone to secure the referee's real views.

12 Can you afford the fees? Choose the consultant and negotiate the fees and other terms and conditions. Do not use fees as the main criterion for the selection – you will get the wrong adviser.

179

7
■ ■ ■

Undertaking the project

The objectives for this chapter are as follows:

■ to help you to prepare for the actual project start;

■ to explain the consultancy process;

■ to show you how to manage the project;

■ to enable you to monitor the performance of the consultant;

■ to explain when and how the project might need to be redefined;

■ to enable you to determine what review processes the project may need.

Getting started
■ ■ ■

Early meetings are very important, including those that take place before the consultants have been commissioned. They set the tone of the project and determine what sort of rapport will be achieved between client and consultant. I find that if we break into laughter during the pre-selection meetings, not only am I likely to get the work, but also the project will be a success because the personal chemistry is already established. (It will also be fun.) The importance of empathy cannot be over-estimated; it is vital.

Indeed, all meetings are important. They provide a vital element of any commission as they encourage understanding and a shared view of the issues. They also provide an essential opportunity to generate opinions and ideas. Through them you and the consultant will be able to work towards shared values, to your benefit and with the result of providing better final recommendations. Without that shared understanding the consultant's recommendation will be difficult to take through to successful implementation, as the solution will not be based on a full appreciation of the values and culture of key individuals and the organisation as a whole.

If the consultant is to achieve early results, it is essential to have an initial planning meeting at the start of any engagement. It is an opportunity to sort out the following:

- What information is available that may be missing from the original brief and any subsequent negotiations or presentations?

- Who will be the client's project manager? When are they available? What is their perception of their role? What background do they have? What expectations do they have of the work?

- What response are staff likely to have to the consultant

or the project? Are there any sensitivities that need to be jointly handled with great care? Do staff have hopes and expectations beyond those expressed by the managers commissioning the work?

■ How is the detailed administration of the project to be handled? You need to clarify any respective responsibilities with regard to secretarial support, etc. (The broad issues should have been set out in the contract or engagement letter.)

Finally, the initial planning meeting should sort out the detailed work plan, at least for the immediate future, so that all parties know what they have to do and when.

In some projects, for instance where the consultant is taking over the project management of an existing project, there may also need to be an initial meeting between the client, the consultant project manager and the suppliers to the project. The requirements of such a meeting are similar to those set out above and it should take place after an initial meeting between consultant and client. In such cases it is particularly important that both client and consultant have a common understanding *before* they meet the suppliers. They need to be singing the same tune.

Continuous dialogue

The initial meeting should only be the start of a frequent and continuous dialogue between yourself and the consultant. Although there will be formal meetings, reports and presentations at various points during a large project, there should be *no* surprises in them for you if you have been closely involved in discussions with the consultant as recommendations have been developed.

The consultant should seek informal contact with you to keep you appraised of new findings or ideas, and to use you as a sounding board or to help interpret what is being discovered. If such informal contact does not happen, then you should be

183

concerned and should find out why not. It may be that the consultant is running into problems that they do not wish to admit; they may be out of their depth, or just blind to the importance of dialogue. It is also possible, although less likely, that the consultant is involved in some detailed technical analysis and feels that there is nothing to discuss.

In my experience during the life of a project there is always something to discuss, even if some of it is only small talk – it is all about maintaining a personal relationship. However often a consultant has brief conversations with a client, there is usually a new piece of information to be gleaned. This might simply the client's considered thoughts from an idea that was sown a week or more ago, it may be some small but relevant detail that the client has just remembered, or it may be new information from a trade association or a meeting with a supplier. There are a thousand and one small but important reasons for talking frequently, even if it is only when passing in the corridor.

184

> *Consultant's tip*
>
> Do not let or cause a professional adviser to take on basic tasks that any competent clerk, or indeed manager, could do. Allow your staff and colleagues time to do the detailed work themselves wherever possible, especially during implementation, and then insist that they do so and meet the agreed timescale.
>
> In this way you will not pay expensive consultancy fees for straightforward work, and you will encourage skills transfer at the same time.

The consultancy process
■ ■ ■

For many forms of consultancy the process is much the same, although there may be additional steps and different approaches to quality control, especially in the technical disciplines such as engineering. For much business consultancy the basic process is as set out below.

What is currently known about the client's problem?

The consultant should identify the problem or area of investigation by carrying out the following steps:

- gather facts;
- quantify the problem;
- research the market, technology or whatever;
- research other people's experience; do not re-invent the wheel.

The consultant should agree the problem with you. They should ensure that you recognise that it is a problem and that it is the right problem. The consultant should then identify possible causes by exploring with you the relationship between the separate elements of the problem, using your knowledge of the organisation and the area under investigation.

185

The consultant should then determine the most likely causes and their effects, and work with you to identify all possible solutions.

What does the client want to achieve?

The consultant should work with you to identify objectives for the short, medium and long term. They should establish relative priorities.

How does the client get from one to the other?

The consultant should decide, with you, on ways to achieve the objectives. They should relate the problems to the objectives, and short-list possible solutions for both the problem and the objectives.

Next, the consultant should decide, with you, which solutions they could achieve, bearing in mind the capability of your organisation with respect to:

- management

- people

- organisation

- technology

- skills

- finance.

You and the consultant will then plan the action to be taken to realise the chosen solution, implement the favoured solution, and monitor, evaluate and revise the plan.

Quality assurance in consultancy

Most consultants and professional advisers take quality assurance seriously. Their reputation is their most valuable tool for winning new business and although it is achieved over many years it always remains fragile. It is often said that a consultant is only as good as their last project; unlike many one-line aphorisms, this one has more than an element of truth about it.

Consultants use a variety of techniques to maintain the quality of their work. The first is their own personal pride and commitment to doing the best possible work for a client. The most basic control is to check regularly that the work that is being done matches the terms of reference. As the final report is being prepared, they should make a final audit of the project's achievement against objectives in the terms of reference. Any omissions should be corrected before the report is finalised or the project finished.

All firms should have procedures aimed at maintaining and raising the quality performance of the organisation. These range from the technical aspects to those important factors such as the receptionists' manner, the speed of responding to enquiries and the ease with which clients can buy the firm's services. As has already been suggested, these may appear peripheral but are, to the client, more visible signs of quality than the technical competence of the work.

In most professional practices of any size there are procedures for work to be reviewed and assessed for quality in the widest sense, from its technical content to its readability. There are essentially two types of review: 'hot' and 'cold'. Hot reviews are performed as soon as the work is completed and before it is sent to the client. They are particularly important where the consultant or the client will be committed, usually financially, once the work leaves the consultant. One would expect, rightly, that a major proposal should be subject to hot review before submission. In most firms it is.

Cold review is undertaken after the event and is intended to be used as a learning exercise and to keep a general eye on standards. The aim should be to learn from the review and to use the knowledge that results from it to raise the performance of the individual and the consultancy firm.

187

Neither review process should be seen as a blame-laying exercise – it will be counter-productive if it is. Rather, hot reviews are aimed at catching mistakes and both types of review are designed to enable learning from each other. By reviewing work the firm as a whole picks up best practice and new ideas and approaches from all its consultants. Properly handled review is a very positive tool.

Reviews can be carried out at two levels: they can be peer reviews or they can be partner or manager reviews of work by junior staff. The approach should be the same – what can be learned from how we did this work? For a sole practitioner the opportunity for mutual reviews is not there. Some of the more professional small practices have arrangements to cross review between firms. I have such an arrangement with a couple of former colleagues who work in their own practices (one large, one small) – our relationship is closer than most as we frequently use each other on our own proposals and indeed provide other skills on projects.

Other elements of the quality process in consultancy come through external audit. These are an extension of the mutual review agreements described above. There are usually formal requirements of professional associations, brokerage services and consultancy networks. The large firms conduct external audit by having offices audit each other, not only for quality but for compliance with the firm's procedures and standards. Often in such cases part of the salary bonus for the partners in the office depends on their score for the standards visit.

The last form of quality check is the client satisfaction survey or visit. Usually performed some time after the work has been completed, a senior person from the consultancy checks that the client is happy with the work that was done and the attitude and approach of the people doing it. I suggest later that the client should also want this review before the consultants finally leave.

If you, as a client, are thinking of using a small firm of advisers who are too small for in-house review to work, ask them what quality control procedures they have. If they can demonstrate review agreements with other firms then you are probably looking at a highly professional firm.

Codes of practice

Most professional bodies have formal codes of conduct for their members, as do the larger firms. These should be binding on the people they cover and there should be some form of disciplinary procedure for complaints with regard to breaches of the code of conduct. Most take a similar form. The code from the Institute of Management Consultants is shown below as a suitable example.

Institute of Management Consultants
Code of Professional Conduct – summary

Principle 1 – Meeting the client's requirements
- A member shall regard the client's requirements and interests as paramount at all times.
- A member will only accept work that the member is qualified to perform and in which the client can be served effectively; a member will not make any misleading claims and will provide references from other clients if requested.
- A member shall agree formally with the client the scope, nature and deliverables of the services to be provided and the basis of remuneration, in advance of commencing work; any subsequent revisions will be subject to prior discussion and agreement with the client.
- A member will hold all information concerning the affairs of the clients in strictest confidence and will not disclose proprietary information obtained during the course of assignments.
- A member will make certain that advice, solutions and recommendations are based on thorough, impartial consideration and analysis of all available pertinent facts and relevant experience and are realistic, practicable and clearly understood by the client.

189

Principle 2 – Integrity, independence, objectivity
- A member shall avoid any action or situation inconsistent with the member's professional obligations or which might in any way might be seen to impair the member's integrity. In formulating advice and recommendations the member will be guided solely by the member's objective view of the client's best interests.
- A member will disclose at the earliest opportunity any special relationships, circumstances or business interests which might influence or impair, or could be seen by the client or others to influence or impair, the member's judgement or objectivity on a particular assignment.
- A member shall not serve a client under circumstances which are inconsistent with the member's professional obligations or which in any way might be seen to impair the member's integrity; wherever a conflict or potential conflict of interest arises, the member shall, as the circumstances require, either withdraw from the assignment, remove the source of conflict or disclose and obtain the agreement of the parties concerned to the performance or continuation of the engagement.
- A member will advise the client of any significant reservations the member may have about the client's expectations of benefits from an engagement.
- A member will not indicate any short-term benefits at the expense of

▶

▶

the long-term welfare of the client without advising the client of the implications.

Principle 3 – Responsibility to the profession and to the institute
- A member's conduct shall at all times endeavour to enhance the standing and public recognition of the profession and the Institute.
- A member will comply with the Institute's requirements on Continuing Professional Development in order to ensure that the knowledge and skills the member offers to the client are kept up to date.
- A member shall have respect for the professional obligations and qualifications of all others with whom the member works.
- A member will negotiate agreements and charges for professional services only in a manner approved as ethical and professional by the Institute.
- A member shall be a fit and proper person to carry on the profession of management consultancy.

190

Project management

■ ■ ■

Once they have appointed the consultant too many clients expect to have no further involvement with the project, except perhaps for the occasional progress meeting and to authorise the consultant's invoices. This is a big mistake – if continuous dialogue is important before the project starts, it becomes even more important during the project.

You, as the client, still need to manage your own staff and to ensure that they are delivering what is needed by the adviser. Even more importantly you should stay in touch with the consultant's findings and thinking. You should know whether the consultant is having any problems, or whether there are any changes needed to the project plan or the terms of reference.

The key areas that you need to manage are compliance with the terms of reference, timescale and budget. The consultant should warn you of any changes in these areas, but you need to give them the opportunity to do so. In fact a consultant *expects* a client to be interested in the project; after all it is the client's problem and they will have to live with the results. It is also the client's money that is being spent.

Consultant's Casebook

One of the most difficult projects I have ever undertaken happened early in my career. It was a small project, less than ten days' work, for a major bank. It was also my first solo consultancy project for a non-group client. We agreed the terms of reference, signed contracts and had an initial meeting to get the project under way. That was the last I saw of any of the people who had commissioned me; I could not even contact them on the telephone. I went from a state of excitement and enthusiasm to despair in a matter of a week. In the end I could not even get hold of the client to tell them that the project was a waste of time! So I did the work from the documentation they had provided (including an earlier report by another consultant with an almost identical brief), sent in the invoice and got on with the next job. What a waste of money by the client!

191

Project manager

You should appoint your own internal project manager or co-ordinator to act as the consultant's principal point of contact. I always include such a requirement in any engagement letter or proposal, as it makes my life easier. For example, I do not have to try to telephone eight other people when I need to set up a meeting with the client's project team – I ask the client's co-ordinator to do it using the internal telephone.

This approach also has considerable benefit for you as the client, as it ensures that there is one person who is well informed and who can report the status of the project at any time. The client project manager should also be able to spot a project that is slipping for any reason and take appropriate action – either internally if colleagues are failing to meet their promises, or with the consultant project manager if there are problems on that side.

The person given the task should have sufficient authority to take day-to-day decisions about the conduct of the project; they should also have rapid access to the highest management level when necessary. Equally important, they should have the time to do the work and to make themselves available to the consultant whenever necessary. It may well be that the consultant will sometimes need five minutes at short notice to clarify an issue or seek agreement on some point so that they can take the project forward.

Similarly, where there is a consultancy team involved on a larger project there should be a senior consultant with overall project responsibility and for account management. They should be readily available to you, the client, and should have sufficient authority and experience to run the project without constant reference to more senior colleagues.

Project planning

A detailed project plan will be required at an early stage by all but the smallest project. An outline plan will have been included in the proposal, but it will need to have more flesh put on it as a result of early meetings between the client and the commissioned consultant. If a formal project planning and management methodology or tool is to be used, then it should have been agreed as part of the contract negotiations or have been required in the bid invitation.

A key point with all project planning methodologies is that each task or step should have a clearly defined output that does not require a subjective judgement; the stated output should be such that it either has or has not been completed. The deliverable element should be such that it delivers a fundamental part of the project. For example, producing the minutes of a meeting would be an objective deliverable, but would not be a fundamental element of the project's implementation so should not constitute a task. Rather more appropriate would be, say, the delivery of new equipment or receiving planning permission for a new building – these are essential elements in the success of the project unlike the production of the minutes which is simply administrative support.

Project planning therefore should focus on what is material to the success of the work, not the process of the work itself. Keep focused on what is important and do not let bureaucracy rule.

At an early stage a good consultant will do the following:

- focus on what is material to the project;

- recognise priorities;

- recognise what is achievable;

- only investigate or analyse what is germane to the project, although they may provide incidental findings with some suggestions for the client to analyse themselves.

As a result the consultant will appear unflustered, and may not even appear desperately busy. Such consultants generally tend to take project and time management seriously – it is the only way of retaining any sort of order in their lives.

193

Poor consultants scatter-gun the job and have little sense of direction; they appear busy but they are not focused.

Consultant's Casebook

CONSULTANCY IS NOT JUST DESK WORK

A team of design consultants were working on the layout of sewers for a water company. The consultants spent weeks poring over maps and talking to engineering companies and suppliers. They made a presentation to the client showing the routes they had designed and, when asked, they were very reassuring to the representatives of the water company that there were no problems of any kind.

The client's project manager asked the lead consultant whether there were any problems along the route with access or with vegetation or whatever. After profuse reassurance from the consultant he dropped a photograph on the table which showed that the proposed route ran under an avenue of trees for as far as the eye could see, and he suggested that there might be a small snag!

▶

▶

> Unfortunately, the consultants had spent little time on site; they had done the work all from maps and plans at their desks. The project manager had detected this and was a little suspicious about how thorough the consultants had been. He made his own inspection of the route. It turned out that they had only visited a part of the route.
>
> The lead consultant turned red and blustered, and the project manager sacked them there and then.

Progress meetings

All project plans should have regular review points between consultant and client to feed back progress and any potential problems or, indeed, opportunities. Apart from the client and consultant project manager these should involve the minimum number of people.

Progress meetings need not be formal and should be short. If they are held weekly, half an hour should be sufficient, unless some particularly complex issues have arisen. The basic format should be a brief verbal report by the managing consultant, followed by discussion on issues arising as a result. It should also be an opportunity for you, the client, to feed in any new information relevant to the project.

The amount of documentation produced should be kept to a minimum; at most the meeting should produce a brief note of key decisions and the essential agreed actions and responsibilities. One page should be sufficient.

If the meeting takes longer than suggested, or if it produces pages of paper, then the effectiveness of the continual, informal communications has to be questioned. The majority of decisions and feedback should be taking place, as required, outside the progress meetings.

> ## *Consultant's tip*
>
> *It can be argued that the value of meetings is inversely proportional to the number of people present – two being best of all. (You cannot have a meeting with one!)*
>
> *Often the most valuable meetings are informal and are held standing up, as a result of a chance encounter in the corridor or by the coffee machine.*

Activity reports

Some consultants routinely provide regular activity or contact reports. However, if the relationship between the client and the consultant is good and based, as it should be, on mutual trust and respect, then these should be unnecessary. Indeed they should not be needed in any case, as the effectiveness of a consultant's input should be obvious from their achievements. Note that we are talking here about routine regular reports of meetings or work undertaken. I do not include in this project task lists or action plans from meetings; these are used to ensure that everyone knows what they have to do and what their deadlines are.

195

The preparation of unnecessary routine reports is time-consuming and therefore expensive. Someone has to pay for them and, of course, that is you, the client. Personally I have never had time to produce them; I am too busy doing the actual project work. I have worked for organisations that used them and I found them an incredible waste of resources, consultants' time, secretarial time, postage and stationery; they were hated by everyone and many clients asked *not* to be sent them.

I believe that in many cases unnecessary reports show lack of confidence by the consultant in the value they are giving to the client. They are then a matter of self-justification. I have never been asked for them by clients, and the need for them seems to originate from within the consultancy profession itself, possibly for some sort of self-protection. I find them a bureaucratic waste of time, as my experience is that clients rarely read them anyway! In some circumstances I suspect that some of my more cynical colleagues may use such reports to give an illusion of activity and to justify charges that are not justified by the quality of the work they are providing to the client.

Nevertheless, a consultant should be prepared to justify time spent on a client's behalf if they are charging on a day-rate basis. Most consultants I know keep a record of where their time is spent and can, if requested, provide a breakdown.

Monitoring the consultant

The emphasis should be on measuring outputs rather than inputs. If the measurable objectives in the project brief and the plan are being met, then you are getting what is required. Is any more monitoring needed? If the consultant is billing fees above the level agreed then it may be worthwhile asking for a breakdown of where they have spent the time. But generally it should be obvious if the consultant has spent extra time on the project.

Remember that a consultant is a self-managing independent practitioner, not a contract member of staff who is paid by the hour. It is my view that there is too much emphasis by employers on measuring the time staff spend rather than the results they achieve. Measuring attendance hours encourages poor productivity rather than increased effectiveness and efficiency.

However, there is a way of avoiding the worry of whether the consultant is putting in the time charged. That is to seek a fixed-price contract or a fee based on the results achieved. It is not appropriate to all kinds of work but, as indicated in Chapter 6, such charging bases are increasingly popular. However they are not necessarily the cheapest solution, as the consultant has to build in a contingency for the risk they are taking; if the work comes in under the estimate the consultant pockets the extra profit. You have to make your own judgement of the risk, and decide whether you are prepared to take it or would rather pay the consultant to carry it.

At the end of the day, as a client, you should be buying results or effective advice, not a number of hours. Measure the outputs not the input, otherwise the consultant may be being rewarded for inefficiency. Do not get bogged down in monitoring the time that the consultant spends on your project. If you are getting the level of advice and the results you built into the terms of reference, then you are getting the value for money that you wanted. Does it then really matter whether the consultant spent ninety-eight hours instead of the hundred that they indicated in their proposal?

On the other hand, if you are not getting the results, then really make the consultants justify the time spent on the project; ask for breakdown by person and date. If you are not getting the results you should already have picked this up and have been pressurising the consultant before it became a serious problem.

Poor project management

As a general rule consultants are good project managers, it is the only way they stay in business. That said, everybody has projects that go wrong sometimes.

Most consultants value their reputation, and their clients, sufficiently to bear the consequences when they get the timescale or resource requirements of a project wrong. They grit their teeth and carry the extra time, resources and other costs of delivering their promises without charge to the client. However, some try to pass their mistakes on to the client. You must watch for this and should not expect to pick up additional costs because the consultant misjudged matters and had to buy in additional help. Similarly, you should not let a consultant drop or modify deliverables to recover their increased costs or to keep the project on track. You should insist on *all* agreed deliverables being delivered to the time and quality standards agreed at the start of the engagement.

197

Always be on your guard for consultants extending the scope of the work without formal agreement. Whilst you should insist on agreed products being delivered, you should also be wary of additional, unrequested items being produced and causing a consequent increase in the bill. Consultants always claim, often justifiably, that they seek to add additional value over and above that agreed in the terms of reference. On a fixed-price contract that is not a problem – additional findings and recommendations outside the scope of the agreed work are at no cost to the client. With time and materials or day-rate contracts you should watch for the 'added value' becoming an added cost. Consultants often seek to 'sell on' further work. Sometimes this is overt, at other times it may be tried by making the implementation of recommendations sound more difficult than is really the case. The first is fine as long as you, the client, are prepared to buy only what you need and want – you must be prepared to say 'No' if you are not contemplating further advisory work.

198

The situation where the consultant deliberately makes the advice more complex than necessary to make you dependent on them for interpretation and implementation is cynical and should be resisted. If your consultant is doing that then use another firm if you need further support. As I indicate elsewhere, it is your responsibility to ensure that you understand what the consultant is telling you. If you cannot, the consultant is duty bound to find a way of expressing the message in a way that you as the client can understand. Do not let the consultant push you into buying further support until you understand what they have already done – then you can make your own judgement as to what, if any, further support is needed.

Mutual responsibility

■ ■ ■

199

Rearranging meetings or failing to undertake agreed work

Inevitably during a consultancy project, you, the client, will want to cancel or postpone meetings for a variety of reasons: for example, pressure of other work, sickness or not having completed agreed work for a meeting.

Sometimes this is unavoidable. However, if you cannot give the consultant due notice so that they can use the time on other projects, then you must be prepared to pay for that time. Obviously there should be some give and take on both sides.

As a general rule, consultants should avoid cancelling meetings except for illness or *force majeure*, rail disputes, etc. To be called 'professional' requires one to be so in all aspects of one's work, including managing a diary. However, if a consultant cancels a meeting they will have to pick that time up later and still deliver the project to time, so there is a sanction of increased time pressure and lost billable time.

Similarly, you, the client, should have due regard for a consultant's busy diary; my diary is usually almost fully booked for a month or more ahead. I do try to leave some space for urgent meetings, meeting new clients and keeping in touch with old friends. If late cancellations or ineffective meetings due to lack of preparation happen too often, then you should expect to bear the cost of the consultant's time.

Understanding and communication

It is a consultant's responsibility to make themselves clear. But on the other hand the client has a matching responsibility to ensure that they understand the analysis, recommendations and anything else the consultant appears to be telling them. If, as client, you feel the consultant is not explaining in a way that you can understand, challenge them to make themselves clear. The consultant has taken on your project to help you resolve your problems – the project is not a private intellectual exercise for the consultant. When asking for clarity do not feel embarrassed at your lack of understanding, but be firm about your right to have the issues explained in a way that is intelligible to you; that is what you are paying for.

200

Consultant's tip

If a consultant or other adviser starts by saying something along the lines of 'Let's make this absolutely clear ...' or 'It is essential that you understand that ...' they will almost certainly be anything but clear. So be particularly concerned that you understand and do not let them hide the issues in a flood of jargon and buzz words.

Feed back your understanding, in your own words, and seek confirmation that you have understood correctly. Keep at it until you have. Otherwise the 'expert' will lose you and you will end up having to take their analysis and recommendations on trust. You will then lack the understanding to carry the project through when the 'expert' leaves.

Finally, with regard to listening and understanding, do make sure you also understand what is *not* being said, or what is only implied. Most consultants, most of the time, are straight-forward and want to be understood. However, sometimes they want, often subconsciously, to avoid admitting problems and will say things that the careful listener will realise are flannel. Get to the bottom of it.

You have paid for knowledge; it only becomes useful if you understand it, so make sure the whole job is done.

Using client staff

You may well wish to use your own staff to work with the consultant as part of the project team. This is key to skills transfer from consultant to client. Knowledge can be exchanged through the vehicle of reports or in presentations, but skills can only be learnt by the client's own staff, by their seeing the skill practised and trying it for themselves, ideally with the support of the consultant.

Working closely together also addresses many of the project monitoring issues. As a result you should have less need for detailed activity reports – your own staff are there to ensure delivery as promised.

As well as the skills transfer, sharing the work also provides a smooth transition into implementation and operation. However, it is essential that the same staff are made available for the implementation phase as were seconded to work with the consultant on the analysis and recommendations.

It is important that the personality and attitudes of the staff used on the project are compatible with those of the consultants. It may be desirable for the consultants to interview and select possible candidates; at the very least the consultant should create a job specification to cover skills, abilities and personalities for the seconded positions. This should be treated like any other recruitment or selection exercise.

The people assigned to the product should have the technical

201

knowledge and appropriate experience of the work involved. The project should not be used as a basic training or learning exercise – the people concerned have to be able to operate effectively at a similar speed and level to the consultants from the start. Otherwise, the project will be slowed and the costs will rise.

As has already been stated, continuity is the key both during and after the consultancy project. That means that the people seconded should be able to give the project all the time it needs and not be dragged away onto other 'higher priority' tasks. If that happens, it gives the advisers just reasons to pass the buck and blame you, the client, for project failings. Where there is a joint client–consultant project team there will always be a temptation for either party to blame the other if the project does not meet its objectives. Joint staffing of a project does therefore add complexity to some areas of management of the relationship, but with goodwill, mutual trust and clear division of responsibilities for the engagement these complexities are manageable.

Other issues

With the increased use of computers, consultants may well wish to share data electronically with you. Be careful about the possibility of the transfer of viruses onto your computer systems. Most large organisations, and many smaller ones, have policies on the copying of data from outside systems onto their own in-house computers. If there is a policy in place then the consultants should adhere to it and it should have been included in the proposal as a requirement. The consultants will probably have their own procedure back at their offices, so they will not be uncomfortable with the need for care.

If you do not have a policy on data copying and you have computers, especially personal computers and portables, then you urgently need to put in place a policy and procedures.

Project review process
■ ■ ■

Once a week, or once a month, depending on the length of the project, the two project managers from the client and the consultant should meet to review progress; others may be present but the number should be as small as possible. This should be a short meeting, usually of less than an hour, to review progress against the project plan.

Normally the consultant makes a short presentation of progress since the last meeting and describes any difficulties encountered or other issues that may be having an impact on progress. The meeting should then seek to address those issues that are proving a block to progress and determine what impact it all has on the project plan.

The project plan should be updated accordingly and the objectives for the coming period agreed to try to keep the project on track. Sometimes the project will slip for perfectly good reasons, and you will have to decide that it is safer to change the target dates than to risk failing to meet the original timescale. Project management is to a large extent a question of managing risk, not simply a matter of bringing a project in on time. Indeed, there can be reasons why keeping to the timescale might increase the risk; for example, a snap General Election could create uncertainties about policy that could alter the required outcome for the project.

Other decisions with regard to the project should be taken in an appropriate forum as they arise. The project review is simply to ensure that the agreed project plan is being met and that the objectives are still valid. If there are significant changes to the timescale and nature of the project, then a more substantial redefinition of the project is required.

Redefining project objectives
■ ■ ■

Often, probably inevitably with strategic or many analytical projects, the terms of reference agreed before starting the project need to be changed. Initial findings may require a project to take a slightly different direction or may identify other issues that need to be addressed first. In such circumstances it is appropriate to revise the terms of reference but if communication with the consultant is working properly the need for the changes should not come as a surprise.

If you need to make changes to the terms of reference then it will probably be necessary to refer these to the original selection committee. They will be aware of the detailed reasoning behind the original structure of the projects. They can therefore help the project managers to determine whether there are changed circumstances in the light of new information, or whether the project team has simply misunderstood or lost sight of the original objectives.

204 Any changes should be by mutual agreement between client and consultant and should be formally documented in writing. The new document should include full details of the implications for costs, both for the project and for subsequent implementation, timescale and client resources. If the changes are substantial I recommend that a full revised engagement letter or contract should then be prepared. In any case the new document should make clear what parts of the original contract still stand and what is additional. In all cases the document should be supported by the new objectives, a schedule of costs and a project timetable at the same level of detail as those originally agreed.

Executive summary

Initial planning is important, and you should make the most of the opportunities you have before you select the consultant. Use this time to develop a mutual understanding and a personal relationship.

Once the consultancy firm has been appointed, hold a meeting to agree the programme of work, to clarify the respective roles of client and consultant, and to sort out the administrative details such as identity cards, signing-in procedures and, most importantly, the location of the coffee machine. This is an opportunity to introduce the consultants to those members of staff with whom they will be working. The meeting should also be used to ensure that the consultant is aware of any sensitive areas.

Throughout I have been stressing the importance of continuous dialogue, and now it must start in earnest. Use every opportunity to exchange information, ideas and even pleasantries. You and the consultant need to build a personal relationship and an understanding of each other's capabilities.

The consultancy process varies from project to project, but it is essentially one of analysis, synthesis and recommendation, followed by implementation. Quality control of professional advice is usually by review, often by one's peers. 'Hot' reviews take place before the client sees the work and 'cold' reviews afterwards, to ensure that standards are being maintained or improved and as an aid to raising them. There may also be external audit to check compliance with agreed standards and to maintain professional membership or accreditation.

205

Project planning and management are much the same as for any piece of work, but should not need to be bureaucratic if the necessary dialogue is working. Both client and consultant should appoint their own project manager to oversee the work and act as the principal point of contact on each side, especially for administrative matters.

The consultant needs to be monitored, but not through measuring input. Rather, you should ensure that they are achieving the objectives and delivering what was promised. It is at this stage that the need for measurable objectives and clear deliverables becomes clear.

You should agree procedures at the outset for project review and, if necessary, redefinition of the project. Such changes in the terms of reference should go back to the original selection committee for approval and should be agreed in writing before any action is taken on them by either party.

Checklist

1 Get the project under way as soon as possible with a meeting to:

   - address administration issues such as key personnel, identity cards, location of facilities, workplace rules, etc;

   - clarify the brief and add any new information that has come to light or changed since the invitation documents;

   - talk through the cultural and political issues for the client organisation and sort out any sensitive areas that need handling with care.

2 Agree the detailed work plan and respective responsibilities.

3 Arrange progress meeting dates and other project reporting requirements.

4 Agree how client's staff are to be used, prepare job specifications and make arrangements for selection if necessary.

5 Start work, but take time to understand each other.

8

■ ■ ■

Implementing recommendations

This chapter takes you through the final stages of the project – through the implementation of the consultant's advice to taking the implementation forward after the consultant leaves. The objectives are as follows:

■ to enable you to handle the final reporting stage of a project;

■ to ensure that you understand how recommendations are made;

■ to guide you through disengagement from the consultant;

■ to enable you to avoid becoming dependent on the consultant.

Final report

■ ■ ■

The contents of the final report should not come as a surprise. It is usual practice for the consultant to make a presentation of their report at the draft stage to the group who commissioned them. Even at the draft stage there should be few surprises if, as I have already discussed, you and your team have been talking regularly with the consultant. You should have been kicking ideas around with the consultant, examining their findings and between you seeking appropriate responses. So the only, little, surprises may be in the detail or the way the information is presented. There should be no substantive points that have not been explored both formally and informally before the report is written.

Why present the report at draft stage? First there is the need to ensure that any factual statements are correct and have not been misunderstood. It is also an opportunity for quality control and to ensure that the thrust of the report fits with the original objectives in the terms of reference and, to some extent, with the expectations of the client.

Making a presentation of the report provides an opportunity to explain some background that may be inappropriate to include in the final published report. It is most definitely not an opportunity to cover up the unpalatable, but it is an opportunity to be sensitive to individual and group issues at the periphery of the consultancy study.

Consultant's Casebook

DEPARTMENTAL REVIEW

An associate conducted a departmental review examining how a department and its procedures worked. It was inevitable, and necessary, that a lot of information about individual members of staff and their opinions was collected and used to make a judgement of the department's effectiveness. Much of the evidence was given, in confidence, because the consultant promised not to attribute it to individuals.

As is often the case, the report was to be published widely within the organisation and it would therefore have been inappropriate to talk about individuals, their strengths, weaknesses and aspirations. However, there was some information that the consultant had that could be shared with the chief executive, department manager and the personnel and training manager who had commissioned the work. Also, the consultant was able to make sensitive recommendations about the development of individuals without compromising confidentiality. This was to the benefit of the staff concerned but was not for general publication or even, in some cases, to other senior managers.

The issues were flagged discreetly in the draft report, which was circulated only to the commissioning team. These issues were used as a prompt and discussed in detail at the presentation of the report to the project group. They were then removed from the final report – not to cover anything up but simply to protect confidences and the individuals.

209

Although the report may be revised as a result of discussion of the draft this revision should only really be of minor matters of detail and of presentation. There may also be some changes to the emphasis to ensure that the intended message is clear. In extreme cases where the consultant has got something significantly wrong, and the client can provide evidence, then the report might need to be amended. This would probably be after the consultant had undertaken further work. If communication works well then such a problem should not arise.

The presentation is *not* an opportunity for the client to cover up the findings or to make recommendations that fit a particular agenda. Most consultants, and all good ones, will not fudge their report for such reasons. Although the stereotypes suggest otherwise, professional advisers and consultants do have integrity and will not compromise it to satisfy a client's ulterior motives. So do not ask them to.

Finally on this point, if the client wishes to publish the report in bowdlerised form then it will have to go out under the manager's name, not the consultant's. In such circumstances I would have no hesitation in denying that it was my report to anyone who asked, even if it lost me further business from that client – I would probably have not been prepared to do it in any case.

Often at this stage the responsibility is in the process of being passed from the consultant's to the client's implementation team. Consequently the client's team will have to solve many of the problems associated with carrying out the adviser's recommendations. However, it is not unreasonable to expect some guidance on implementation from the consultancy work.

When reviewing the final report the client, and the consultant for that matter, should consider whether the following points have been covered:

- In proposing solutions, and probably an approach to implementation, has the consultant considered likely and possible problems and discussed them with the client?

- In doing so has the consultant suggested ways of addressing the problems, should they arise?

The final part of most consultancy reports is a costed action plan of some description. This should form the basis of an implementation plan for the recommendations. For some projects the final output is a detailed project plan for implementation – it all depends on the terms of reference and the nature of the work.

The plan ought also to identify the key members of the client's staff who have been involved in the consultancy project and who, whilst doing so, have been prepared by the consultant to take the project through implementation. The necessary skills should already have been transferred to members of the commissioning organisation's staff. Before the consultant finishes it would be useful to check that the required knowledge and skills have been passed on. If they have not, and this was in the terms of reference, then the consultant still has some work to do. If this was not a requirement then the client should consider whether they need to buy some training to cover the shortfall; they should be more careful with the terms of reference next time.

Consultant's tip

Not only should you make sure that staff have the appropriate skills and knowledge, but you should also ensure that there are staff with the skills, knowledge and enthusiasm to sell the project to their colleagues throughout the organisation.

The content of the plan is described in the following paragraphs.

The action or task

The task should be described in sufficient detail for the client's implementation team to understand it. The client is probably going to have to manage the implementation, so the report and the associated action list should stand on their own and not need further reference to the adviser.

It is imperative therefore as part of the discussions on the final report that you, the client, *fully understand* the report and actions. As has been said before, the client has to take responsibility for understanding the message being given to them by the consultant. Both parties can only be sure that it is understood by each checking with the other.

The consultant has a responsibility to make the message clear by writing clearly and by presenting the findings and recommendations in a form appropriate to the client. They should then check, by questioning, that the message has been passed across in the intended form. We have all played Chinese whispers at parties, and it is great fun, but there is too much at stake to play games with our work and businesses.

You, the client, also have a responsibility to make sure that you have understood the message properly. If there is anything in the report or presentation, *however basic*, that you are not sure about you *must* clarify it. If you find yourself in that position in a meeting you will usually endear yourself to your colleagues by asking the 'dumb' question. I have often watched great smiles of relief pass round the room when someone has overcome their embarrassment to ask the question that everyone wanted to raise but was afraid to ask. Take comfort from the fact that it is the consultants who have not made themselves clear. You are only protecting the consultants from their failure to get their intended message across to your colleagues!

As with any project planning, a task is a piece of work with a clearly defined product; it is not simply a sub-process. The deliverable item must be such that there is no doubt that the work is completed.

The person or persons responsible for ensuring it is carried out

As with any project plan, there has to be someone with the responsibility, and the right level of authority, to ensure that it is achieved to time, cost and quality. They might not undertake the majority of the work themselves, because they will delegate it, but it is their reputation on the line if it fails for any reason.

I would like to stress that appropriate authority *has* to go with responsibility. Too often I see junior managers given the responsibility to deliver part of a project without sufficient authority to take the decisions to make it happen. They have to keep running back to their boss for the decisions; that costs time and almost certainly dooms that manager, that task, and possibly the project, to failure. Someone who has sufficient authority and *still* seeks confirmation is not ready for the responsibility, needs counselling and guidance about their role or is being expected to do too much and should be moved elsewhere (within their competence) for both their own and the project's good.

The deadline for that task

If there is no deadline for a job then it is likely to be late. As a general rule I meet tight deadlines, but I struggle with a loose or ill-defined timetable. I am far more likely to be late with the latter even though I work hard to avoid procrastination.

So the deadlines should be tight but achievable and designed to give the project as a whole an appropriate momentum. There may be need for pauses in the project for contingency and to allow consolidation of what has been achieved. If change is too continuous and too fast then a form of fatigue starts to afflict the staff subject to it and they become less and less able to respond. So do not target all your change into one area of the organisation; give time for change to assimilated. Then move forward again.

Your advisers will have made suggestions about the timetable, but it is your management who will have to see it through. Make sure you agree with the timetable, seek to have it changed if necessary (through sound argument, not coercion) and make it yours.

Recommendations

The recommendations in a report by an adviser are just that. (There may be a few exceptions where the client has been *required* to use advisers, perhaps by their bank, but this is not the general case.) It is management's responsibility to decide on the course of action and to carry it out. The consultant will accept changes up to a point, but even if they are not prepared to move as far as you, the client, would like in changing the report, you can, and should, make your own decisions. You and your staff will have to live with the consequences; the consultant will not.

Budget
■ ■ ■

At least an outline budget should be prepared for most action or implementation plans. It is usually necessary to do some costings to decide between alternative courses of action and these should be shared with the client. This will allow the decision to go forward to be made 'in principle' with detailed costings and planning to be undertaken before the final decision.

As with the action plan, if these are only in outline then you should develop both the project plan and the budget into a fully costed, detailed form. Only at that stage should you make the decision to proceed.

214

Getting staff behind the project
■ ■ ■

Throughout this book and elsewhere much has been made of the importance of ownership and of getting staff behind the project. At no stage is it more important than at the implementation stage, because the staff concerned will have to carry it through after the adviser withdraws. It is therefore imperative that wide staff involvement starts at the earliest possible opportunity – ideally at the stage of defining the challenges facing the organisation.

If you and your consultant leave involving staff until the recommendations have been made then it will be an uphill struggle to get them to give more than grudging support to the implementation and subsequent operation. Basically, if you have left the staff issues until now you have left it too late.

Information

Through whatever channels you have available, share as much information as you can about what the consultants are doing. Staff will often believe that they are not getting all the information even when they are – mistrust is a too common aspect of management–staff relations. If you are open staff should at least see that you were being honest, albeit after the event.

Where possible give staff the opportunity to meet the consultants and explore the project with them. Encourage staff to use informal meetings and other opportunities to seek information about what is happening. A client of mine once admitted that he had a problem, summed up for him by a colleague as the fact that no one talked 'shop' when they had an opportunity for small talk. He felt, and I agree, that this was probably part of the key to their communication problem.

215

The key points that you must communicate are what the consultants are looking at, why, and what the overall objectives for the work are. Also make it clear that ideas and information from staff will be regarded as valuable and, if they wish, can be contributed on a non-attributable basis if they are made directly to the consultant.

Basically, give as much information as you possibly can and give opportunities for staff, especially those directly affected, to discuss the project with both the client managers and the consultant.

Newsletters

Colleagues who specialise in communication audits tell me that a staff newsletter is one of the surest signs that an organisation has a communications problem – some of my PR colleagues might not like that! Staff often regard newsletters as a joke, do not read them and leave the editor with an uphill struggle in getting material to fill them.

I have seen newsletters used to support projects of all types and they rarely work. They tend to be too general, too superficial and not sufficiently topical. Different groups need different information at different levels and no standardised form of communication will satisfy all audiences.

Meetings

Meetings are the bane of a consultant's life, as in many organisations they are an excuse to avoid acting or taking decisions. It has often been said that the most efficient form of government is a benign dictatorship, and the same is true of meetings. The smaller the meeting, the more effective it usually is.

CNN, the satellite and cable news television network, has to take a lot of decisions during any working day to adjust schedules to respond to rapidly changing world events. Nearly all their meetings are held standing up or on the move; their meeting rooms do not have chairs! They have been one of the fastest growing television companies anywhere in the world.

Too many meetings are attended by too many people and last too long. In many organisations there is a tendency to think, 'If I do not attend this meeting what am I missing?'. That may arise from the internal politics of the organisation or be a matter of implied status for the individual. In my meetings I want those attending to ask, 'what can I contribute?'. If the answer is 'nothing' I do not want them there; they will get in the way and they have a job to do elsewhere.

Genuine involvement: use their knowledge openly

Where you are using information from staff meetings, individuals or wherever, make sure that it is acknowledged and that due credit is given. Many people have a tendency to take the credit for contributions from their staff (but pass down the brickbats) and I know from experience that this is very demotivating. It does not encourage people to participate.

So if you are seeking your staff's ideas you should acknowledge and share them with others and give credit to the group or individual who originated them. The attitude you are seeking to create is that you are all in this together and that, if the organisation prospers, you all do, one way or another. Everyone wants to be associated with success.

This recognition of the contribution of individuals has been adopted in a slightly surprising way by many companies developing computer software. In many packages, even from the biggest manufacturers such as Borland and Microsoft, a non-documented sequence of keys will bring up on the screen the names of everyone on the project team. And when I say everyone, I mean everyone, including the trainee who made the coffee. In some cases they have even included a thumbnail picture of individuals who have made particularly special contributions. A little bit of recognition goes a long way.

217

Consultant's Casebook

OVERCOMING RESISTANCE

One consultant (in this case an internal one) found a cheap but very effective way of rewarding and encouraging the production staff in a large textile factory to meet their production targets with regard to volume, rework, scrap, etc. For each week in which they achieved their targets he put the coffee machines on free vend. This worked for a variety of reasons:

- it was convenient – they did not have to scrape around for small change;

- it was recognition;

- it was an additional benefit.

Perhaps the biggest motivator was that it was something the factory workers got that the office staff did not. The consultant fought very hard with the board that it should stay that way. Production staff had always felt that they tended to be ignored when it came to perks – now they had one of their own and which they had achieved through *their own* efforts.

▶

▶

> It was not the financial benefit (or indeed the cost to the company) that was important. It was the less tangible things that it said about recognition, respect and so on.
>
> Of course, when the production staff did not achieve the expected performance they had to start buying their own coffee again. As a result they could not take the perk for granted and treat it as a right! They got very cross with themselves when they lost it and really worked to win the perk back. It achieved more than was ever expected of it.

Managing the implementation

■ ■ ■

Project management is as important at the implementation stage as it is during the consultancy project itself. Most organisations have managed projects of various kinds themselves – the tools are no different because it is, or originated as, a consultancy project.

As with the consultancy work, the key tasks need to be identified with measurable objectives. Monitor the achievement of those objectives against the plan and success will follow. The process has been outlined already, and there are many good books on project management for those who wish to know more. The principles are the same whatever the discipline.

Do we still need consultancy support?

■ ■ ■

It is at this stage that you will probably be coming to the end of the original project. Even if you have anticipated a further phase to cover implementation, you should not roll straight into it. Use the end of the recommendation stage as an opportunity to review the whole of the next step.

I would recommend that as the draft recommendations are published you take your in-house project team aside and start the whole selection process again, beginning by defining the new project and its objectives. Once you have done that you can then decide a) what support you need, if any, b) the nature of such support, and c) the likely cost and availability.

Only after you have done this would I suggest that you make any decisions about using the existing consultants for the new work. If they have the appropriate skills and are available then they will have significant advantages as a result of their detailed knowledge of the project to date. If you wish to use them then you will need to negotiate terms of reference for the new work, just as you did with the original project. Unless your standing instructions expressly forbid single tenders, you will not need to go through the whole process of inviting bids from a short list. Even the EC/GATT regulations for public procurement recognise this situation and accommodate it by not requiring the follow-on work to go to open tender (as long as you are not trying to get round the rules by breaking the work up into several small projects below the threshold).

219

If you do need, for whatever reason, to go to tender then the process is a repeat of the previous selection. There is one convention: it is usual to include any incumbent firm of advisers who are suitable on the short list, unless of course it is their failure on the previous work that has caused you to invite bids for the next stage.

Bear in mind that most consultants will want their work to be successfully implemented. Apart from professional pride, a successful implementation makes for a better reference. It also means that they have a greater chance of being invited back to do other work. Therefore they will usually be willing to give some informal and occasional advice after they have moved on to other things. Usually, if it is a very occasional and brief telephone call, they will make no charge. They will put the cost down to creating goodwill. If such advice becomes more than that, then there should be an exchange of brief letters detailing the basis for it and the fees that have been agreed.

Executive summary

The final report has to be understood by the client and it is the client's responsibility to ensure that they do. The consultant has a responsibility to write clearly and in language appropriate to the client. As part of making sure that everybody is clear about the implications of the findings and recommendations a consultant will usually discuss the report in draft form.

This review at draft stage is not to make substantial changes to the recommendations or to hide anything that has been discovered. It is simply to ensure that the client understands the report and that the way it is written makes that understanding possible. It may be necessary to alter the emphasis slightly to make sure that the message is communicated as intended and is not distorted by insensitive language. The review is not for making any material changes of emphasis or content.

The final report should normally contain a costed action plan, at least in outline, which should already have been established as affordable.

Checklist

1 Does the report deliver what was required in the terms of reference?

2 Does the final report reflect your understanding of the discussions with the consultants during the project? If there are any surprises, examine why.

3 Does the report contain a clear statement of the action that needs to follow – whether or not the consultant is to be involved?

4 Do you, and will your staff, understand the report's findings and recommendations?

5 Is the style of the report and its emphasis appropriate to the expected readership?

6 Have any inappropriate personal or commercially confidential details been removed from the version for wider circulation? If it is very sensitive have all relevant people received and signed for a numbered copy?

7 Do not try to browbeat the consultant into making fundamental changes to the report unless they have not complied with the terms of reference. Consider what the implications of covering up the findings will be, especially if the consultancy refuses to put its name to the report to protect their integrity.

9
■ ■ ■

Into the future

The objectives for this chapter are as follows:

- to enable you to disengage the consultants smoothly;

- to enable you to avoid becoming dependent on the consultant;

- to enable you to understand the importance of a final review of any project;

- to ensure that you recognise that change is continuous and unrelenting;

- to help you to welcome the excitement of change.

Letting go

■ ■ ■

At some stage you will have to let the consultants go. If the relationship has been fruitful and strong personal relationships have developed, it can be difficult for you to say goodbye. But it must be done. Consultants are there to undertake a particular piece of work and they expect to move on when it is completed.

If the terms of reference have been written properly it should be obvious when the work commissioned has been completed. Some projects may not be clearly defined, for all sorts of reasons that we have already discussed, and these can easily find new reasons for continuing. You know the sort of thing: 'We must just do xyz before ...'. On these sorts of projects the client has to end the relationship. If nothing else they need to give themselves time to absorb the changes that have happened during the project, decide what is still to do, redefine where their priorities lie and, perhaps, what support might be needed.

If any further assistance is required then the whole problem definition and adviser selection process should *start from the beginning*. As a result of the work with the external agencies the organisation should be facing a very different set of issues than when it set out. Management and staff will need time and space, away from the influence of their advisers, to decide what response *they* need to make to the new circumstances.

Consultant's tip

Good consultants do not need to leave work undone to make clients dependent on them. They will finish the work, tell the client they have finished, and know that the client will recommend them and use them on future projects as

> *appropriate. They are in the business for the long haul and look to maximise fees over their career.*
>
> *Poor or inexperienced consultants may rely on spinning the work out for longer than necessary to maximise short-term fees. They may do so because, in their heart, they know you will probably neither recommend them or use them again. They need to maximise fees over the short term.*

Final project review
■ ■ ■

Before the consultant finishes you should sit down with them to make a final, formal review of the project. This serves several obvious purposes: it ensures that everything has been completed, and it provides for handover of information, documents and responsibilities.

There is a lot more that can be gained from the final review. It is an opportunity to conduct a final audit not only of the selection process but also of the management and execution of the work. By using the final meeting as a learning experience, a key requirement for all work using consultants, you should improve the ways in which you do things in the future. You will raise your game and so will the consultant.

Some of the matters that need to be covered at that final review meeting are as follows:

- What are you going to do with the recommendations?
- How was the project handled by both sides (and how can you do it better next time)?
- Did the project meet its objectives?
- Were you satisfied with the consultant's work?
- How did the individual consultants perform?

If the project was undertaken by a team, the managing consultant ought to conduct an assessment of each member of the consultancy team with the client group. This will then form part of that person's routine appraisal and help to identify personal development opportunities and needs for them.

These last two matters should form a basic part of the consultant's quality assurance process. Be concerned if the consultant does not address these issues at all.

What else was achieved along the way?

Most consultants that I know get inordinate satisfaction from watching a client develop. When this happens the consultant has to work at a higher and higher level for each project to stay ahead of the client's growing skills. Much of the time consultants work well within their abilities because their clients cannot cope with more. Most find any opportunity to work at the edge of their knowledge and intellectual capability both exciting and highly motivating. I certainly do, and by doing so I learn a lot very quickly!

Never-ending need for innovation and change
■ ■ ■

Continuous cycle of control

For an organisation to succeed, it should be subject to a continuous cycle of control. The process of planning, action, monitoring and control is a continuous loop. What is more, it is a loop that runs faster and faster as time goes by – so your planning and change processes have themselves to change to keep up.

Innovation – the core competency

I have already referred to Peter Drucker's assertion that innovation should be any organisation's core competency. You cannot gain competitive advantage from simple incremental improvement, because it is not fast enough. You certainly cannot gain any significant edge over your competitors by copying what they are doing – that way you will *always* be playing follow-my-leader.

You need to make jumps in your capability before the competition make them, and there is no one whom you can copy! You have to be able to innovate, either on your own or by using creative advisers and consultants. Unfortunately, it appears, according to the *Financial Times* (12 September 1995), that '... they [management consultancies] have largely ceded the 'guru'·field to business school academics, many of them with little hands-on experience'. I have to agree that this is a problem at all levels within management consultancy (and I suspect the same is true for many other areas of specialist advice as well). I see a lot of very hackneyed, even old-fashioned, thinking when I visit clients and read previous consultant's reports. I suppose it is inevitable that, as the industry has grown, an increasing number of the people within it are merely competent journeymen rather than creative thinkers. If you find a consultant who is imaginative, practically minded and, above all, enthusiastic, hang on to them, and give them as much work as possible to keep them away from your competitors!

Consultant's tip

If the ideas coming from your adviser do not make you feel uncomfortable, then they are not pushing you fast enough. The changes they are proposing are not sufficient to give you real performance gains.

If the consultant is being genuinely creative then the ideas will feel uncomfortable. If you are to be a winner you cannot be comfortable or complacent. Read the case study on page 228 Having to do it all again next year – that director was making real gains, the process was not very comfortable for him or his staff, but he knew he had to do it.

New ideas can also feel uncomfortable because they are wrong. However, be honest; do not use that as an excuse to stay in a comfortable rut.

Running hard, even to stand still

Even for your organisation to stand still, let alone develop, you have to run hard to stay with your competitors. It does not matter whether you are a commercial organisation, or a public-sector or other not-for-profit body – you still have competitors competing for the same grants, funding or work. You too cannot stand still if you wish to survive, let alone succeed.

So this project is finished. Breath a big sigh of relief and get the next change programme under way.

Becoming world class

To become world class in some aspect of your business is a great achievement but it is not the end. Whilst you have been making the changes necessary to achieve that success, your competitors have been overtaking you in other areas. You will still be chasing hard to stay up with them – the only consolation is that they are having to work as hard at it as you are.

Consultant's Casebook

HAVING TO DO IT ALL AGAIN NEXT YEAR

A friend who is an operations director of a company in a large textile group had the pleasure of taking a group of his staff to a major group awards presentation in London. They had won the group's award for quality achievement.

They all enjoyed the meal and the presentation, and the director made the acceptance speech on behalf of his company and its staff. Everybody adjourned to the hotel bar where the partying continued. Colleagues from other group companies came and congratulated them, but everybody was concerned that the director, normally very outgoing and a party animal, was remarkably subdued. He seemed especially subdued for someone who had been fêted earlier in the evening. Surely he had an excuse to let his hair down?

When challenged, the director told friends that, looking at the excitement of all his staff, he realised that he had got to tell them on Monday that they had got to do it all again next year, and the year after! They were going to have to go through all the soul-searching and hard work all over again. It was as if their success counted for nothing.

He knew what being world class meant.

Where do we go from here?

■ ■ ■

If letting go is too difficult, or if it leaves you feeling just too insecure then consider an alternative to having a consultant effectively running the next step for you. As we discovered early in this book, many consultants are used to taking on a variety of roles, some project-based, some rather more personal. In this case, think about retaining someone, not necessarily the recently departed consultant, to act as a sounding board or mentor. It may avoid the need to get a consultant in to take on a full-scale project. It will develop your own skills and confidence and will cost a lot less.

The person chosen should have wide experience, knowledge and perception, as well as some understanding of your work. You will need to have mutual respect for each other for the relationship to be fully effective. If your relationship with the consultant was excellent, then they may well be the right choice. They will certainly understand the challenge you are facing as they helped to create it!

If you go down this route, agree a small (very small) retainer with a day rate for work above that. If you genuinely use the mentor as a sounding board rather than as a member of the team you will find (if you are up to your job) that you are using them for less and less and at a higher and higher level. I have just come to the end of two years with one client on this basis (the subject of the case study on page 4 *Growing*

Together). We ended the arrangement because he was finding it difficult to use a day a quarter! We will carry on having occasional meetings and discussions, but more as friends and peers, until we discover a project that we both need to work on together (which could even be for a third party).

This is a role I quite often take, either formally or informally, and it can work very well – I recommend it.

Au revoir or Goodbye?

■ ■ ■

You have had your final meeting with the consultant; is that the end? Not necessarily. Like many consultants, I like to take an interest in how my projects and clients have developed after I finish my work with them. I will stay in touch with clients, especially if the relationship has worked well on a personal level. Once in a while I may give them a call to talk through what is happening, how they see their business developing, and to talk about their industry in general. If appropriate I might arrange to pop in and see them (always with prior notice) and perhaps even have a light lunch with them.

This is part professional curiosity and part good business for both myself and for the client, who will probably get some free advice or at least some new ideas to do with what they will. I get feedback on how my recommendations have worked in practice or how they have had to be changed to reflect industrial or market changes. We can also swap information about mutual areas of interest and appreciate how things look from different perspectives. It helps both the client and myself to broaden our thinking.

A good consultant takes an active interest in their specialist fields and should be aware early of developments in those fields. Successful consultants also take an active interest in their clients' businesses and business in general. As part of staying in touch with clients I send them any bits of relevant information that I believe they will probably not have seen. If you receive such items from an adviser that you have used in the past you can be reasonably sure that they take their own personal development seriously and read widely to do so.

If you receive any snippets of useful information from me, then file them and put me on the shortlist for your next project! Seriously though, you will already know me if you are getting such items as I only send them to people I have had dealings with, probably at least by being short-listed for a previous project.

Checklist

1 Disengage from the adviser in a controlled way and seek to retain informal contact whatever else might be decided.

2 Do not let the consultant make you dependent on them; they should make it possible for you to carry the work forward on your own.

3 Make the last task a formal review of the way the work has been handled from both sides. It should be a learning process, not an opportunity to apportion blame for any problems. Both parties should learn something from any project.

4 Start planning the next phase in your organisation's change programme and, if necessary, start collating a long list of consultants …

5 I think this is where I came in.

Appendix A

■ ■ ■

Glossary

Buzz words Jargon, especially fashionable jargon words. Some are useful shorthand; many are contrived.

Conflict of interest Something the consultant has to keep quiet from both clients! Seriously, a good consultant will avoid them.

Engagement A contract for an assignment that may be project-based, or for advice as and when required.

Engagement letter The formal letter confirming the terms of an engagement. It is the contract to provide the services described in the letter.

Expression of interest A pre-qualification stage before inviting full proposals from a short list. Often used in public-sector procurement to ensure open bidding but to allow screening to produce a short list of invited bidders.

Facilitator Effectively the chairperson of a discussion group. A facilitator should hardly be noticed but will steer the meeting's discussions into the areas under investigation. They will help the meeting to achieve its objectives with minimum input. The facilitator will guide a meeting by asking open questions rather than by making statements.

Foot soldier The consultancy equivalent of the chorus line. On projects using several consultants foot soldiers will do the detailed work and prepare the reports and presentations under the direction of the managing consultant.

Invitation to tender The formal document describing some service for which the client wishes those invited to submit formal proposals.

Managing consultant A term often used for senior consultants who act as project and/or account managers. Often a consultant one step down from a director or partner of a professional practice. They will usually oversee the analysis and recommendations.

Mentor Someone who supports and guides on a peer basis. A mentor helps the person being supported to achieve their objectives through sharing their own experience and knowledge.

Rainmaker A high-profile consultant, usually with a well established reputation as an expert, who often sets the tone for the firm. The rainmaker will only work on the highest level projects, usually in an advisory role.

Principal consultant A senior consultant with substantial experience, usually one step down from a partner or director. Equivalent to a managing consultant in most cases, but a principal consultant may be a high-level technical specialist with no management responsibility

Managing partner In a professional firm, the partner who takes day-to-day executive authority for the management of the practice. The equivalent of a managing director or chief executive in a corporate body. Note: not necessarily the senior partner (who will often be chairperson).

Appendix B

■ ■ ■

Further reading

There are many sources of related reading matter published. Whilst most of it is not aimed directly at the reader who is looking for advice on choosing consultants much is still relevant. The books reviewed briefly here all have something to offer the would-be client.

How consultants work

These books give an insight into how consultants are being advised. They will give you a consultant's eye view.

Starting a High-Income Consultancy
James Essinger, Pitman Publishing, 1994

A very readable book aimed at the new independent consultant probably making the transition from a management role to that of external advisor.

High Income Consulting
Tom Lambert, Nicholas Brealey, 1993

One of the best-selling books on developing a consultancy practice. It is very readable and gives an excellent insight into professional practice.

How to Make it as a Consultant
William A. Cohen, Amacom, 1990 (UK distributor – Management Books 2000)

Another book aimed at the independent consultant starting out on their new career.

Management Consultancy
Clive Rassam and David Oates, Mercury Books, 1991

∨ The first half of this book is a history of the development of management consulting, illustrated by interviews with senior business leaders. The second part gives the history and ethos of several of the major international consultancy firms.

Handbook for the Scientific and Technical Consultant
Dr R. Gordon Booth, Management Books 2000, 1995

This is a guide for creating and running an independent consultancy practice with the emphasis on scientific and technical consulting.

Management Consulting
Milan Kubr (ed.), International Labour Office, 1986

∨

This is perhaps the definitive work on the practice of management consulting. It is heavyweight, both in size and content and, whilst the serious investigator might wish to dip into it, I would not recommend that clients buy it. I suspect few consultants, even those who have it on their bookshelves, will have read it from cover to cover.

Internal consultancy and self-help
■ ■ ■

The Successful Manager's Guide to Business Planning
David Freemantle, McGraw-Hill, 1994

A business planning work book aimed at the practising manager.

Marketing Plans
Malcolm McDonald, Butterworth-Heinemann, 1995

A comprehensive book that covers both the theory and a practical approach to developing marketing plans. It includes a fast track planning workbook.

Every Manager's Guide to Business Processes
Peter G. W. Keen and Ellen M. Knapp, Harvard Business School Press, 1996

This book sets out to demystify business process re-engineering and the many related topics. It provides a useful tool to enable the reader to cut through the jargon and hype associated with business transformation.

Re-engineering your Business
Daniel Morris and Joel S. Brandon, McGraw-Hill, 1994

Whilst many books have concentrated on the theory of re-engineering this book provides a framework for the application of re-engineering. It is not light reading but it does provides an insight into implementing major change.

Benchmarking for Best Practices
Christopher E. Brogan and Michael J. English, McGraw-Hill, 1994

Benchmarking and learning from one's competitors is an essential part of being a leader in one's industry. This book is a valuable handbook for any manager faced with making their organisation 'world class'.

Succeeding with Change
Tony Eccles, McGraw-Hill, 1994

This book is a guidebook to managing change. It addresses all the important issues including caring for any casualties; a topic that is often overlooked.

Other guides to choosing professional advisers
▪ ▪ ▪

Getting the best from agencies and other outside services
Geoffrey Smith, Kogan Page, 1994

This book is specifically aimed at the client looking for advisors on promotional aspects of business including public relations consultants, advertising agents, direct mail consultants and exhibition services.

Getting Value from Professional Advisors
Catriona Standish, Kogan Page, 1993

An easy read with particular advice on choosing professional advisors such as solicitors, accountants and auditors.

Managing Consultants
Igor Popovich, Century, 1995

A slim guide to using consultants.

General Management Thinking

■ ■ ■

Reading some of the following will give you an insight into the thinking behind many consultancy offerings. By being aware of the ideas in these books, you will be better equipped to detect hot air from possible consultants. Knowledge is power. If you understand current management and business thinking you will be in a position to see whether the consultants' approach is soundly based or whether they have twisted the ideas to continue to sell their out-of-date offerings!

If you wish to dip into some of these books, bear in mind that many of them are academic in tone and do not make light reading. They generally justify the effort required if you have an interest in management thinking.

Re-engineering the Corporation
Michael Hammer and James Champy, Nicholas Brealey, 1993

A readable book from the people who coined the term 'business process re-engineering'. Perhaps not the seminal work they would like to claim, but important none the less. Any professional manager ought to be aware of what business process re-engineering really is, as it has been hijacked by many other interest groups, especially the computer systems industry.

The Empty Raincoat
Charles Handy, Hutchison, 1993

Charles Handy provides a challenge to everyone to face the many paradoxes and conflicting needs that are faced by individuals, organisations and society itself. Understanding those paradoxes will enable us to work towards resolving them through our organisations and personal careers. By doing so we will have the opportunity to succeed.

The Discipline of Market Leaders
Michael Treacy and Fred Wiersena, Harper Collins, 1995

The ideas in this book are easily understood and would appear to give a sound basis for any business seeking to reposition itself to respond to the new uncertainties in the market-place. Carrying them to fruition may be a bigger task, however.

Process Innovation
Thomas H. Davenport, Harvard Business School Press, 1993

Process Innovation links re-engineering and information management. It provides an action-oriented guide to using information technology to enable re-engineered process to work.

The Re-engineering Revolution
Michael Hammer and Steven A. Stanton, Harper Collins, 1995

This is a follow-up to *Re-engineering the Corporation* and is written by one of its authors; it seeks to explain the process of re-engineering.

239

Re-engineering Management
James Champy, Harper Collins, 1995

This book is by the other half of the *Re-engineering the Corporation* duo. It sets out some of the reasons why business process re-engineering has failed so many businesses or has not delivered the significant benefits that were promised.

Creative Destruction
Richard L. Nolan and David C. Croson, Harvard Business School Press, 1995

Creative Destruction sets out a six-stage process for transforming business and clarifies many of the issues related to re-engineering of business.

Appendix C

■ ■ ■

Example engagement letter/ terms of reference

Mr J Smith
Managing Director
ACME Development Co. Ltd
...

Dear John

Review of finance and IT department - Structure and processes

I set out draft terms of reference for the above assignment as a result of our meeting last Tuesday and a subsequent telephone conversation with your chairman, Jill Jones. We can discuss them further if necessary.

I have included an outline of where the initial work may lead - however these terms of reference are for Stage 1 only. The terms of reference for Stage 2 should be redefined in the light of the findings of Stage 1.

Objectives

The objectives of Stage 1 of the assignment are:

- to determine whether the finance department is structured in an appropriate form for the demands placed upon it;
- to determine the skills (competencies) required by the finance department and to identify any gaps and consequent training needs;
- to understand why the finance department always seems to be under pressure despite staff working hard - in particular to understand whether the department has the total resources it needs to perform the functions demanded of it;
- to make an initial comparison of skills, salaries and functions with other departments in both commercial and other development companies;
- to recommend how the IT function should be organised, what skills it requires and where it is best placed within the organisation;
- to identify where there may be opportunities for improvement in efficiency and effectiveness in the way finance services are delivered;

- to suggest strategies for realising the opportunities for improving performance;
- to identify any immediate performance improvements that may be made and associated training or staff redeployment that may be needed;
- to complete Stage 1 of the project by 11 August 1995.

The objectives for Stage 2 will, probably, be to:

- redesign processes to realise identified opportunities for performance improvement;
- identify staff, training and system needs to support those new processes;
- satisfy other objectives as agreed with the Management Team or identified as part of Stage 1.

(Objectives are clearly stated so that they can be tested, by the consultant, as part of their own internal quality control, and by the client, as part of the management of the project and their procurement processes. There is a clear timetable for project management by the client and the consultancy.

With Phase 2 both the consultant and the client are looking forward to the future.)

241

Our Approach

In Stage 1 Solidus will examine both the processes adopted by the department and the attitudes and skills of all staff, including the Finance Director. We will also consider the demands placed on the department by other managers and the demands placed on those managers by the finance department.

We will:

- interview the management team to ensure that we understand the culture and values of the organisation;
- use a mixture of structured and informal interviews with all members of the finance department to understand their perceptions, personal strengths, ambitions and motivations. We will also seek to understand their expectations for this review;
- run a session with the whole group to see how they work as a team;
- interview users of the service to see whether it meets their expectations and needs;
- interview all departmental heads to get their views on the nature and quality of the service provided by the finance department and to understand their relationship with both the team and individuals;
- work with the Personnel Manager to review the organisation structures and procedures to which any recommendations will have to fit;
- examine and document some of the key processes to determine effectiveness and efficiency;

- record any other findings that fall outside the scope of this project but which we believe the management should be aware of. Where appropriate we will make recommendations as to our view of the appropriate response;
- analyse our findings and prepare a brief report summarising the findings and our recommendations for further action;
- present our findings to the management team and discuss with them what further steps should be taken.

Note: whilst we will prepare a final report there should be no surprises in it as we will wish to discuss our findings and responses with appropriate directors throughout the project.

In Stage 1 this will be an overview to identify the main issues and where best to apply resources to improve effectiveness and efficiency. Stage 2 will seek to examine those processes etc. in more detail and, if necessary, to redesign or, where possible, to eliminate them.

(This section has set out a guide to the process to be adopted by the consultancy in undertaking this project; this will give the client a feel for what will be required of them.)

Our Role

Solidus will:

- interview all finance staff to determine perceptions (of both themselves and the department), attitudes, etc;
- interview users of the service provided by the finance department in other departments to appreciate their views of the service and to gain some understanding of their expectations and needs;
- examine key processes identified as a result of discussions with staff; in particular we will consider the delays in the system by comparing processing time to total elapsed time for those processes;
- liaise closely with the Personnel Manager; and other senior managers as appropriate;
- produce a brief report summarising the findings and recommendations;
- present the findings and recommendations to the management team;
- report through the Managing Director.

Your Role

ACME Development Company will:

- provide access to finance department and other staff;
- provide appropriate documents, such as the business plan, corporate strategy and any reviews of organisational and pay structures that may be relevant;
- provide access to, or with our guidance analyse, timesheets for all departments;
- provide facilities for private interviews.

(These sections make clear the respective responsibilities of the consultant and the client so that there is no confusion or dispute over who does what. They also give the client guidance as to the internal costs of the project.)

Fees

Our initial estimate for the work involved will be approximately 11 days for Stage 1, although this may depend on the amount of comparative work required. If, as the work progresses, we determine that the project might take more than 11 days we will discuss this with you, before incurring the extra work, to see how it might be mitigated. The subsequent Stage 2 will be subject to a separate estimate, but is likely to be a series of sub-projects which can be costed individually. Some aspects of Stage 2 may be addressed as part of redefining procedures to support the new finance systems and will form part of that project.

We would propose to charge £*yyy* per day for this (and related) work, to include all expenses involved in travel between our offices and the ACME Development Company's offices in Cardiff. Other travel will be charged at 50p per mile (your standard rate) and all other expenses at cost. Value Added Tax will be chargeable on all items at the appropriate rate at the date of invoice.

This would result in an estimated fee for Stage 1 of around £*z,zzz* plus VAT.

The fees due for work undertaken will be invoiced on completion and payment will be due, in full, by the end of the following month.

243

(Note: this is an estimate, not a fixed price, but there is a provision to warn the client that costs are rising (for whatever reason) and to give them the opportunity to take appropriate decisions to manage the costs. Also is clear what costs are included and what additional costs are not included. (In this case the day rate is effectively all-in except for genuinely exceptional items - perhaps to visit another organisation considered an exmple of best practice.

The billing and payment terms are clearly stated and form part of the contract.)

Our Team

The work will be directed by Martin Wilson, who is an experienced management consultant and has worked with you and the company on several occasions. He will be supported on this project by Tim Evans, who is an experienced senior consultant, with particular expertise in staff development and quality systems (including both Total Quality Management and ISO9000) and who, as a non-executive director of a manufacturing company, is introducing Investors in People. Tim will undertake the majority of the work and will be your principal contact for this project. Tim's full curriculum vitae is attached.

Martin and Tim will have access to other specialist consultants (in-house and external, as discussed) whom they will be able to call upon as the project demands. Such staff will be contracted to Solidus and will be bound by the terms of this engagement letter. Their fees and the quality of their work will be the responsibility of Solidus and are included in the above proposal.

(This section clearly identifies the key members of the team who will actually undertake the work. It also states the basis on which other specialists may be used.)

References

As you know, it is not our policy to publish names of clients or details of the work we have undertaken for them without their permission. However, David Jones, Chief Executive of Zed Development (telephone: *xxxx*) has agreed to act as a referee.

I am sure you will also have spoken to your auditor, Michael Moxon, and as you probably know, we have done similar work for several of their clients, in some cases in collaboration. Michael understands our capabilities very well.

We were originally introduced to Acme Development by Jim Jackson at Apex Properties, and as you will know, we have carried out a similar departmental review for them although in that case it was not in finance.

(References are provided but only by prior permission so as to maintain client confidentiality. It would not be usual to list clients and projects without permission. A good advisor takes client confidentiality very seriously and the most they might publish is a list of organisation types (e.g. a private hospital, an engineering company), perhaps their size and the projects undertaken - but only if by doing so they cannot be attributed to a particular organisation.)

Intellectual Property

Solidus reserves all rights with regard to copyright or patentable inventions produced as part of this project. The client is licensed to use such copyright material or inventions for its own internal use only. All such copyright material must include a copyright notice in the following form: ' © Solidus Limited, 1995, All Rights Reserved'. It must not publish or allow to be published such material without prior written permission from Solidus Limited.

(This section is not particularly applicable to the example terms of reference, but it is necessary in many situations. For example, if part

of the project was to develop a general purpose training course that the consultant wanted to use, albeit in slightly modified form, they would need either a licence from the client, if they were given copyright, or, as here, to retain the copyright themselves. The need to include the copyright notice is a necessary additional protection for both client and consultant in case the material is used by others without permission.

Generally the client will not need to own the copyright if they have been licensed to use the material for the agreed purposes. If they wish to own the copyright then they should expect to pay an additional fee, although practices will vary from profession to profession.

Similarly, designers may wish to retain patents for themselves although it may be more appropriate to assign the patent rights to the client with an obligation to maintain and protect the patent. In return the consultant may get a royalty on sales (possibly not on the original product) or on additional uses or licences. Maintaining a patent in global markets is very expensive and both parties need to think hard about whether they can afford and justify doing so. Again the whole position on this will vary from case to case.)

245

Use of Reports

All reports produced as part of this project are for internal use of the client only. They must not be used in external discussions or external negotiations or divulged to third parties without prior written consent from Solidus Limited.

(In this case the use of the report is not an issue, as the project only concerns internal management issues. In many cases reports may contain judgements on the market opportunities or financial strength of the organisation, in which case the client may be tempted to use them in negotiations with the bank or other third parties. If the bank then uses the report to support a decision it has effectively made the consultant or professional advisor a party to that decision.

If the client envisaged using the report for such purposes, then this should have been made clear as part of the terms of reference. It may result in higher fees, because the consultant may need to be even more rigorous than for internal purposes. The consultant and client both need to balance the risk of getting figures or decisions wrong with the cost and delays of getting a more reliable result. If third parties are going to base decisions (especially financial ones) on the report, then the risk to the advisor is much increased.

All that said, in most cases the use of reports is not an issue and, where it becomes desirable for the client to give the report to say, their bank, then permission is usually given. It may be that the consultant would wish to send a complete copy directly, possibly, with a covering letter explaining any limitations in the report or the work behind it. In such a case the client should have sight of the letter before it is sent so that they can decide not to use the report if they wish.)

I hope this meets your requirements. Tim and I look forward to discussing it with you when we meet you at your offices at 9am next Wednesday …

(The client gets to meet the key team members before the project is started.)

Yours sincerely

Martin Wilson
Managing Director
Solidus Limited

Enc: Solidus Limited - Profile

Curricula Vitae:

- Martin Wilson
- Tim Evans

The above letter accurately states our understanding of the work to be performed and the fees, terms and conditions that will apply. We therefore wish to proceed with the work as described and this copy, duly signed, constitutes our acceptance of the above terms.

Signed: Date:

Position:

For:

(The engagement paragraph is normally included on the final agreed terms of reference - it would be rather presumptious to include it on the initial draft proposal!)

Appendix D
■ ■ ■
Example invitation to tender

Summary

For brevity and to avoid duplication the summary is omitted here. In your final document there should be a one- or two-page summary of the key points and requirements of the full document.

Introduction

XYZ plc is seeking consultants to assist with the redefinition and statement of its corporate strategy to support the next stage of the company's development. The project will have to be completed in only five months and to a very high standard.

Background

XYZ Limited was started in 1986 by Simon Jackson as a high technology research organisation specialising in the origination and development of new products for the consumer market. The products it develops are licensed, in the main, to international manufacturers who sell them under their own brand names. It has a considerable investment in patents and other intellectual property rights for leading edge technology for its inventions, including those that have not proved suitable for its existing consumer product clients.

The company grew rapidly and was floated in 1991 as XYZ plc with a valuation of £50 million. At the time it had a turnover of £9.3 million and pre-tax profits of £1.7 million which grew to £23.2 million and £3.1 million by 1993.

The success was based on the highly personal vision of Simon Jackson and the small technical team who founded the company. Unfortunately, Simon Jackson was killed in a flying accident at the end of

1993. Since then whilst turnover has grown to £26 million, profits are down to £1.2 million and further profits warnings have had to be made.

The Chairman, Christopher Davidson, is acting as Chief Executive and he is undertaking a major strategic review of the business. The project described here will form a part of that exercise.

Staff numbers have grown from 127 at the time of flotation to 163 now. The staff are mainly graduate engineers, scientists and designers working in research and development. The administrative staff is small, as is the sales and marketing team - in total they are 43 people including the full-time directors.

In the United Kingdom the company operates from a single site on the Piltdown Science Park where it sited its new building in 1990. The building will accommodate 250 staff and the company is increasingly using telematics to allow the use of staff based anywhere in the world. It has two small satellite laboratory and marketing offices in Japan and the USA. As a result of the recent problems it has deferred plans for further satellites in Germany and Australia.

Definitions

The following definitions are used in this document:

'Consultant' The successful bidder who is commissioned to undertake the work described in this document as amended by subsequent negotiations.

'Contract' The legal contract covering this project and related issues.

'Desirable' Items described in this way are considered important to the success of the project, but there may be some flexibility on the degree of compliance or provision by the bidder.

'Essential' Items described in this way must be fully met by the bidder.

'Project' The package of work described in this tender and as amended by the successful bidder's proposal and subsequent negotiations.

Project definition

Background

XYZ plc finds itself in its current position due to a variety of factors. Most notable is the loss of a strong and charismatic founder. Simon Jackson had a clear vision for the business which was clearly understood by all staff. Since his death the company's vision has become blurred and staff no longer have a clear sense of direction.

This loss of purpose has been compounded by the pressures of being a public company. In particular, the need to achieve short-term gains despite being in a business which is generating new technology which takes time to come to market in the form of consumer products. Further difficulties are created by the need to be more open as a public company and to satisfy analysts when, by its very nature, our work is secret.

At the same time the business has grown rapidly and the management and cultural issues may not have kept pace. It is recognised that keeping a high level of communication and understanding between all a staff is difficult in such circumstances. There have also been the related difficulties of globalisation and the need to achieve some common focus across widespread locations and amongst staff from different cultural backgrounds.

Finally, there is a need to make better use of XYZ's intellectual property which has not been licensed. The patents are expensive to obtain, maintain and protect especially on a world-wide basis. These assets are growing and becoming a drain on profitability.

Objectives

Therefore the objectives are to:

- develop a purpose that:
    - reflects the values of staff, shareholders, customers and our communities;
    - will give a new impetus to the next phase of the companies development;
    - that can be shared with all stakeholders;
    - meet the expectations of the markets.
- quantify the costs and benefits of that purpose and determine what it will mean for the future of the business in terms of:

- turnover;
- profit;
- staff numbers and skills;
- capital requirements.

Deliverables

As the timetable is tight we anticipate much of the reporting will be informal. If this work is to be effective it is essential that findings and recommendations will be fed into our strategic planning work at the earliest opportunity. To this end the consultant will report fortnightly to the Chief Executive and the project manager - much of the reporting will be verbal or through concise briefing papers.

The key deliverable items are:

- a clear definition of direction and core values for the company,

- a costed strategy for sharing, and if necessary fine-tuning, that direction with:
  - staff;
  - shareholders;
  - customers, and
  - the communities of which we are part.
- investment appraisal for the strategy.
- project plan and outline budget for implementing the strategy.
- terms of reference for the implementation stage.

Timetable

The Chief Executive is working to a very tight timetable so as to be able to announce the new vision for the company at the Annual General Meeting in July next year. This project must therefore be complete by the end of March to give time for its conclusions to be built into the Strategic Direction to be put before the shareholders at the AGM.

Organisation

As XYZ plc already has an extensive communications network with many of its staff working from home, the base location of the consultancy is unimportant as the successful bidder will be expected to make use of that resource. It is central to many of XYZ's internal communications.

Because of the importance of this project a dedicated room will be provided with computers and appropriate links to the shared systems. Conference and other facilities which may be needed are available on site and can be booked by the consultant.

The consultant will report their findings and recommendation only to the Chief Executive, Christopher Davidson and his Personal Assistant for the Project, David Jackson. David Jackson will act as project manager for XYZ plc and will be the first point of contact for all administrative matters in relation to the project.

Tender rules

Closing date

All tenders must be received by XYZ plc at the address below:
Consultancy Tender CT/001
Room 101
XYZ plc
Newton Way
Piltdown Science Park
Sometown

251

by 12 noon on Wednesday, 21 September 19*XX*.

Form

All bids must be securely sealed in a plain package with no identifying marks other than the above address and reference.

Warning: Any bids that do not comply with the above rules will not be considered.

Format of document

The proposal document should be structured as follows:

Summary - no more than one page to include:

- Approach
- Key benefits
- Timetable and phasing

- Total fees for the project including all expenses.

Your understanding:
- of XYZ requirements and issues
- of external factors

Approach

- philosophy and emphasis
- methodology
- phasing of the work
- involvement of XYZ staff

Benefits to XYZ

- of using you
- of your approach

The key benefits should be expressed in measurable terms.

Outline project plan

- timetable
- consultancy input
- XYZ resource requirements

Fees and other costs

All fees, costs and other expenses should be aggregated into a single all-inclusive total. All fees and costs should be identified and itemised.

Please provide a breakdown of the time input for each member of the consultancy team, their day rate and all their other related costs.

Personnel to be used
Please provide an outline curriculum vitae for all members of the consultancy team. Only include those members who will undertake 5% or more of the work.

Indicate what special abilities they will bring to the project and how they will contribute to the benefits to be provided to XYZ.

Other information may be provided as an appendix. Please note we are looking for concise proposals so it is in a bidder's interest to include only highly relevant information.

Selection process and timetable

The proposals will be assessed on 22 and 23 September 19*XX*.

Those bidders invited to make a presentation will be advised by 5pm on 23 September 19*XX* of the time of their presentation.

Presentations will be on 4 October. Evaluation will be made 4 and 5 October.

The favoured bidder will be advised on 5 October and be invited to a meeting to negotiate the final details at 9am on 7 October 19*XX*.

It is intended that the contract for the project will be awarded by 11 October and the successful bidder will be expected to start on the project on Monday, 16 October 19*XX*.

Equal opportunities, etc.

XYZ plc is an equal opportunities employer and requires its suppliers to have similar policies. The bidder must state its policy on equal opportunities.

253

Collusion and inducements

The consultant must certify that it has not made, and will not make, any gifts or gratuities to any member of the staff of XYZ plc or its advisors.

The consultant must certify that it has not entered into any pricing agreement, cartel or other arrangements with any other organisations with regard to pricing or bidding for this contract.

Intellectual property rights

Copyright and all other intellectual property rights in original work created for the execution of the Project shall belong to XYZ plc.

The consultant agrees to assign to XYZ plc all rights, titles and interests in and to any inventions and any confidential information made, originated or developed as part of the execution of the Project.

The consultant shall not have the rights to use any reports, data, drawings or other material prepared for the Project for its own commercial purposes except by obtaining written permission from a director of XYZ plc and then only upon such terms as may be imposed.

Workplace rules

XYZ plc is a non-smoking company and smoking is permitted nowhere within the buildings or the perimeter of the site. The consultant and its staff will be required to respect this rule.

Identification badges with photographs are required by all persons working on the XYZ plc site; these will be provided unless the consultant can provide similar badges acceptable to XYZ plc.

Indemnity and insurance

The bidder is expected to have insurance cover for third-party claims of £250,000 for any damage caused by a member of its staff whilst on our premises.

The bidder should also have professional indemnity cover of £500,000 for this project.

The bidder may be called upon to produce insurance certificates to prove the existence of such cover.

Confidentiality (and publicity)

The consultant must not advertise or publicly announce that it is supplying services to XYZ plc without prior written permission of a director of the company.

The consultant, its employees, agents and sub-contractors shall at all times keep secret and confidential all information and other matters acquired by the consultant in connection with the project.

Data Protection Act

The consultant is reminded of the duty to protect data in accordance with the provisions and principles of the Data Protection Act 1984 and in particular to ensure the reliability of staff having access to the data.

Insolvency

XYZ plc may at any time by notice in writing summarily terminate the contract without compensation to the consultant in any of the following events:

- if the consultant, being an individual, or where the consultant is a firm any partner in that firm shall at any time become bankrupt. or shall have a receiving order, administration order or interim order made against them …
- if the consultant, being a company, shall pass a resolution, or the Court shall make an order, that the company shall be wound up (except for the purpose of amalgamation or reconstruction), or if an administrative receiver on behalf of a creditor shall be appointed …

Law

The contract shall be considered as a contract made in England and be subject to English Law.

255

■ ■ ■

Useful addresses

Association of Quality Management Consultants International
4 Beyne Road, Oliver's Battery, Winchester SO22 4JW
Tel: 01962 864394   Fax: 01962 866969

British Computer Society
1 Sanford Street, Swindon SN1 1HJ
Tel: 01793 417417

Business Links
See Yellow Pages.

Chartered Institute of Management Accountants
63 Portland Place, London W1N 4AB
Tel: 0171 631 5309

Chartered Institute of Marketing
Moor Hall, Cookham, Maidenhead SL6 9QH
Tel: 01628 524922   Fax: 01628 531382

The Chartered Institute of Public Finance and Accountancy
3 Robert Street, London WC2N 6BH
Tel: 0171 895 8823   Fax: 0171 895 8825

The Chartered Institute of Purchasing and Supply
Easton House, Easton the Hill, Stamford, Lincolnshire PE9 3NZ
Tel: 01780 56777   Fax: 01780 51610

Computing Services Association
Hanover House, 73–74 High Holborn, London WC1V 6LE
Tel: 0171 405 2171   Fax: 0171 404 4119

The Ergonomics Society
Devonshire House, Devonshire Square, Loughborough LE11 3DW
Tel: 01509 234904

Institute of Management Consultants
32-33 Hatton Garden, London EC1 8DL
Tel: 0171 242 2140   Fax: 0171 831 4597

Institute of Management
Management House, Cottingham Road, Corby, Northants NN17 1TT
Tel: 01536 204222   Fax: 01536 201651

Institute of Data Processing Management
IDPM House, Edgington Way, Ruxley Corner, Sidcup, Kent DA14 5HR
Tel: 0181 308 0747   Fax: 0181 308 0604

Institute of Directors
Mountbarrow House, Elizabeth Street, London SW1W 9RB
Tel: 0171 730 4600   Fax: 0171 730 6335

The Institution of Electrical Engineers
Savoy Place, London WC2R 0BL
Tel: 0171 240 1871   Fax: 0171 240 7735 (general)
                      0171 497 2143 (technical)

Institute of Chartered Accountants in England and Wales
Chartered Accountant's Hall, Moorgate Place, London EC2P 2BJ
Tel: 0171 920 8100   Fax: 0171 920 0547

Institute of Chartered Accountants in Scotland
27 Queen Street, Edinburgh EH2 1LA
Tel: 0131 225 5673   Fax: 0131 225 3813

Law Society
113 Chancery Lane, London WC2A 1PL
Tel: 0171 242 1222

Local Enterprise Companies - Scotland
See Yellow Pages.

257

Management Consultants' Association
11 West Halkin Street, London SW1X 8JL
Tel: 0171 235 3897

National Council for Voluntary Organisations
Regent's Wharf, 8 All Saints Street, London N1 9RL
Tel: 0171 713 6161   Fax: 0171 713 6300   Minicom: 0171 278 1289

Regional Development Agencies
See Yellow Pages or local authority.

Training and Enterprise Council - England and Wales
See Yellow Pages.

Evaluation model

Multiple-level weighted option assessment system

I have used this method for evaluating offerings from many suppliers and found it very flexible. It will expand quite happily from a simple single-level model for a small project to five or six levels and probably beyond. I would recommend using a computer spreadsheet both to develop the model and for scoring each proposal.

Building the model

First develop a list of the main headings under which you wish to evaluate the proposals (this will probably reflect the structure of the invitation to tender and the required format for proposals). Then spread 100% across them on the basis of their relative importance, for example:

1	Company	15%
2	Understanding	25%
3	Approach	20%
4	Expertise	20%
5	Timetable	10%
6	Costs	10%
	Total	**100%**

These percentages are the weights or factor that will be applied to the scores for each heading.

The next step is to break each of the headings down into sub-headings and repeat the exercise at the next level down. For example:

1 Company
1.1	Attitude	50%
1.2	Financial stability	30%
1.3	...	20%

As before 100% is spread across all the sub-headings under each heading, in this case Company. The process is repeated for each heading and each level down until the end of each leg consists of an independent item with no further elements. These final elements are the questions which are scored; all the others are calculated as intermediate values on the way to the overall score.

So we might have:

1 Company (100%)
   1.1   Attitude (50%)
         1.1.1 **Responsiveness** (30%)
         1.1.2 Cultural compatibility (70%)
               1.1.2.1 **Shared values** (25%)
               1.1.2.2 **Compatible with managers** (25%)
               1.1.2.3 **Compatible with staff** (30%)
               1.1.2.4 **Compatible with customers** (20%)
   1.2 **Financial stability** (30%)
   1.3   ... (20%)
         1.3.1 ... (50%)
         1.3.2 ... (50%)
2 Understanding (25%)
etc...

Note that at each level the weights add up to 100% for all the items within the category above.

Create a score sheet consisting of just the scoreable elements with none of the other factors to cloud the issue. The lowest level items, the scoreable items, are in bold above; they can occur at any level in the model.

Scoring

The actual scoring of each proposal can be handled in two ways.

1 Each member of the assessment scores each proposal on score sheet. The scores are then averaged and applied to a final score sheet which is used for input to the overall model.

2 The panel meet and for each item to be scored come to a consensus for the points to be awarded and recorded on the score sheet. These are then applied to the model.

Scores should be consistent and I would recommend using a range from 0 = totally unacceptable, no compliance to 10 = perfect, full or exceptional compliance.

It is important, especially in (2) above, that the scores are only applied to the model after all proposals and all scores have been determined. This will help prevent bias being applied to an instinctively favoured choice. Such bias cannot quite be eliminated by this process but it comes close – I have seen some very surprising results, which turned out to be right, from this formalised approach.

Scoring in the evaluation model works from the bottom up. Each of the lowest level items within a heading are scored by applying the weight to the score awarded. This is then totalled for all the items within the heading to give that score for the heading. This is done for each heading.

As the scoring moves up the model, the input scores and those that have been calculated from a lower level have their weights applied. The new totals are the score for the next heading up. This is repeated until a final single score for the overall model is determined.

			Score	Weighted Overall
1	Company (100%)			
	1.1	Attitude (50%)	6.94	3.47
		1.1.1 **Responsiveness** (30%)	6	1.8
		1.1.2 Cultural compatibility (70%)	7.35	5.145
		1.1.2.1 **Shared values** (25%)	8	2.0
		1.1.2.2 **with managers** (25%)	7	1.75
		1.1.2.3 **with staff** (30%)	8	2.4
		1.1.2.4 **with customers** (20%)	6	1.2
	1.2	**Financial stability** (30%)	9	2.7
	1.3	... (20%)	...	
		1.3.1 ... (50%)	...	
		1.3.2 ... (50%)	...	
		... 1.n		
2	Understanding (25%)		...	
etc ...				

The scores in bold are entered values from the score sheet. The other scores are intermediate scores calculated from lower level entries. For instance the score for 1.1 Attitude would be made up of the entered score (6.0) for 1.1.1 Responsiveness multiplied by its weight of 30%, the calculated score for 1.1.2 Cultural compatibility (7.35, being the sum of the weighted scores 1.1.2.1 to 1.1.2.4) times its weight of 70%. In other words:

$$(6 \times 30\%) + (7.35 \times 70\%) = 5.945$$

The score for 1 Company would then be the total of the weighted scores from headings in the next level down i.e. 1.1 to 1.n. This would be 1.1 Attitude (3.47) plus 1.2 Financial stability (2.7) plus all those to 1.n.

It should be noticed that if the scoring range for each item on the score sheet is between 0 and 10 then all the calculated heading scores, before their weights are applied, will be in the same range. If they are not then there is an error in the weights, and they will not add up to 100% within a category. The final score too will be in the same range.

The best score then is the winner. If I use a spreadsheet I would only display scores to one decimal place at most – there is no need for spurious accuracy. After all you should be looking for significantly different scores; if the differences in scores are in the decimal places then either the evaluation model is too crude or more likely both proposals are equally good.

It takes a little while to set up but the speed with which it produces a definitive result makes it worthwhile. It is actually easier to do than to describe. I commend it to you.

Other uses

I have also used a variation of this sort of approach for assessing options when working on strategic or business planning projects.

Free offer

If anyone would like a copy of a (very) basic model for evaluating a consultancy proposal then please send your business card or your business letterhead with a SAE to:

Getting the Most from Consultants – Disk Offer
Solidus Limited
11 Sandringham Drive, Beeston, Nottingham NG9 3EA

Please note that this model is unsupported and unwarranted and is only supplied on that understanding. It is intended simply to provide an example and starting point to allow you to develop your own version. It requires Lotus 1-2-3 version 3.0 or later; there will also be an alternative Excel version on the same disk.

263

Appendix G
∎ ∎ ∎
References

BOGAN, C E and ENGLISH M J, 'Benchmarking for Best Practices', McGraw-Hill, USA

BOOTH, R G 'Handbook for the Scientific and Technical Consultant', Management Books 2000, UK, 1995

CHAMPY, J, 'Reengineering Management, The Mandate for New Leadership', Harper Collins, USA, 1995

COHEN, W A, 'How to make it big as a consultant', Amacom, USA, 1990

DAVENPORT, T H, 'Process Innovation, Reengineering Work through Information Technology', Harvard Business School Press, USA, 1993

DE BONO, E, 'Water Logic',Viking, UK, 1993

DRUCKER, P F, 'The Information Executives Truly Need', Harvard Business Review, January-February 1995

ECCLES, Tony, 'Succeeding with Change', McGraw-Hill, England, 1994

FREEMANTLE, D, 'The Successful Managers' Guide to Business Planning', McGraw-Hill, UK, 1994

HAMMER, M and CHAMPY, J, 'Re-engineering the Corporation', Nicholas Brealey, UK, 1993

HAMMER, M and STANTON, S A, 'The Reengineering Revolution, The Handbook', Harper Collins, USA, 1995

HANDY, C, 'The Empty Raincoat', Hutchinson, UK, 1993

KEEN, P G W and KNAPP, E M, 'Every Manager's Guide to Business Processes', Harvard Business School Press, USA, 1996

KUBR, M (ed.), 'Management Consulting', International Labour Office, Geneva, 1986

LAMBERT, T, 'High Income Consulting', Nicholas Brealey, USA, 1993

MCDONALD, M, 'Marketing Plans, How to Prepare Them: How to Use Them', Butterworth Heinemann, UK, 1995

MORRIS, D C and BRANDON, J S, 'Re-engineering Your Business' McGraw-Hill, USA, 1993

NOLAN, R L and CROSON, D C,'Creative Destruction', Harvard Business School Press, USA, 1995

POPOVICH, I S, 'Managing Consultants, How to choose and Work with Consultants', Century, UK, 1995

RASSAM, C and OATES, D, 'Management Consultancy, the inside story' Mercury, UK, 1991

SHAW, G B, 'Maxims for Revolutionists'

SMITH, G, 'Getting the Best from Agencies and other outside services', Kogan Page, UK, 1994

Standish, C, 'Getting Value from Professional Advisers', Kogan Page, UK, 1993

Treacy, M and Wiersema, F, 'The Discipline of Market Leaders', Harper Collins, USA, 1995

Index

■ ■ ■